Carreg Gwalch

Best Walks

in

Pembrokeshire

Paul Williams

based on his published volumes:
Circular Walks in North Pembrokeshire
Circular Walks in South Pembrokeshire
Best Pub Walks in North Pembrokeshire
Best Pub Walks in South Pembrokeshire

First published in 2014

© Paul Williams

© Carreg Gwalch 2014

ISBN: 978-1-84524-223-7

Published by Gwasg Carreg Gwalch, 12 Iard yr Orsaf, Llanrwst, Wales LL26 0EH
tel: 01492 642031   fax: 01492 641502
email: books@carreg-gwalch.com
website: www.carreg-gwalch.com

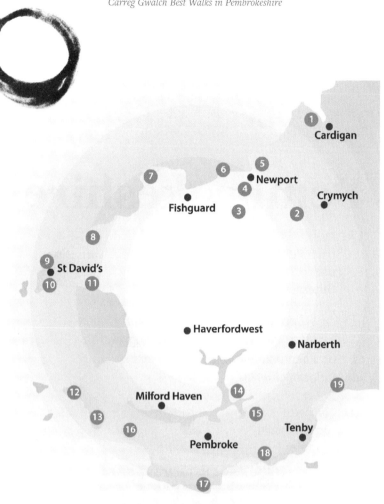

Location of the walks in Pembrokeshire

Contents

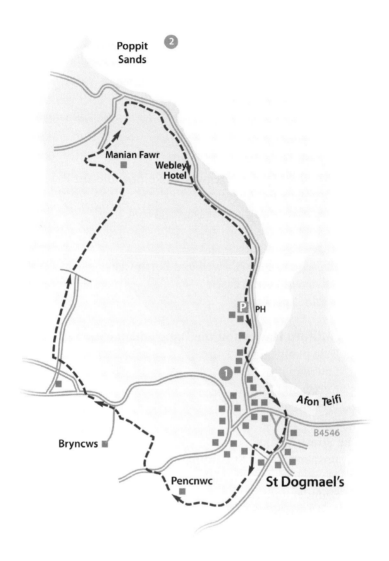

Poppit Sands

Manian Fawr

Webley Hotel

Bryncws

Pencnwc

St Dogmael's

Afon Teifi

B4546

PH

Walk 1
St Dogmael's and Poppit Sands

Walk details

Approx distance: *6.25 miles/10 kilometres*

Approx time: *3½ hours*

O.S. Maps: *1:25 000 North Pembrokeshire Outdoor Leisure 35*

Start: *The Moorings, close by the Ferry Inn St Dogmael's.*

Access: *St Dogmael's is on the B4546 road leading to Poppit Sands from the main Cardigan road. Bus 405 the Poppit Rocket and bus 407 stop at St Dogmael's en route from Cardigan to Poppit Sands. The bus stop for the start (and end) of the walk is the Moorings.*

Parking: *Parking just past the Ferry Inn (on the road leading out to Poppit Sands from the centre of town), at the side of the road by the landing stage opposite the residential street of the Moorings. There is a car park in the village itself, well signposted. Car park also at Poppit Sands.*

Going: *Moderate – minor road, river path, green lane, field.*

1. St Dogmael's (Llandudoch)

St Dogmael (or Dogfael) is believed to be the 6th century grandson of Prince Ceredig, who gave his name to Ceredigion, the Welsh name for the county of Cardigan. There are dedications to St Dogmael in Brittany and Anglesey. Evidence from Christian crosses found near the medieval abbey, and from early writings, suggest that his settlement was a Celtic monastery, either at the abbey's site, or else close by. The Welsh name for the village, Llandudoch, may derive from an unknown saint to whom an early church may have been dedicated, possibly there was another dedication to St Dogmael. Along with St

St Dogmael's Abbey

David's and other monastic churches along the Welsh coast Llandudoch was attacked and sacked by the Norse in 988.

By the 12th century the old Welsh hundred of Cemaes, roughly covering a large part of the Preseli area, was under the not entirely secure overlordship of the Norman fitz Martin family, who ruled from first their castle at Nevern, and then from Newport. Following conquest came piety and it was the Norman habit to follow conquest with the establishment of a place of worship. The established Celtic monasteries with their own unique customs were not to the new lords' liking, and with the newly reformed French orders in mind Robert fitz Martin chose to establish a monastery based on one of these new orders. In 1113 he visited the mother abbey of Tiron in France, returning with thirteen monks and a prior. Some five years later he visited Tiron again, returning with another thirteen monks and permission to raise the priory to an abbey, which appears to have been formally accomplished in 1120. At around the same time a Benedictine priory was founded at Cardigan. The abbey was well endowed by fitz Martin with lands in Pembrokeshire as well as further afield in Devon. His mother gave Caldey island, it's monastery becoming a dependent priory. The late 12th century saw the establishment of two other priories, at Pill near Milford Haven, and another in county Wexford, Ireland. The Tironian order had been established for those who desired a stricter interpretation of the rule of St Benedict, with a greater emphasis on manual labour and an insistence that a monk should be a skilled craftsman. Tironian monks initially wore a grey habit, later changing it to black. Whilst the order had nearly a hundred foundations in France, it's success in Britain was limited, and whilst there were abbeys in Scotland St Dogmael's was it's only abbey in England and Wales. Fortunes varied for the abbey, at one time it gained a reputation for licentiousness, and, despite improvements, by the time of the Dissolution in 1536 the abbey was a poor reflection of it's founders' aspirations. Still discernible from it's first phase of building, during the first half of the 12th century, are parts of the east and west range, and areas of the abbey church. Other remains survive from a number of modifications and rebuilding – there was a major rebuilding programme in the 14th century, possibly required because of damage during the Edwardian conquest of Wales. The present church of St Thomas the Martyr dates from 1847, with abbey materials on site being utilised for the building of the vicarage and coach house in 1866. The church houses the Sagranus stone, dating from the 6th century, and inscribed in both the Latin and Ogham alphabets (Ogham an Irish alphabet using cut lines to indicate letters) with a dedication to *Sagranus, son of Cunotamus*, a local chieftain.

By the late medieval period a settlement had developed outside the abbey, with an established market. The monks had rights to a fishery on the Teifi, and there are early references to salmon fishing and to Seine net fishing. By the 18th century St Dogmael's had developed into an important herring fishery, and by the late 19th century, with the help of trade along the Teifi to neighbouring Cardigan, the village had grown. At the heart of it's economy was the fishing for salmon and sea trout, or sewin, in spring and summer,

St Dogmael's

7

herring in autumn and winter. Widely used around Britain, particularly in estuaries, seine net fishing involves the use of a plain wall of netting which is rowed out (nowadays an outboard motor is used) from shore on a semi-circular course, whilst one of the crew remains ashore holding a rope attached to one end of the net. Once the net is taut the boat returns to shore and the net hauled in. Most of the village's pre 20th century housing stock dates from the 19th century onwards, with modern housing tending to the periphery. One distinctive, and attractive, feature of some of the houses are alternate bandings of Teifi slate and brown stone.

The village, or at least parts of it, were at different times either part of Pembrokeshire or Ceredigion, and in the days when Ceredigion was dry on a Sunday (ie the pubs were shut) the Pembrokeshire pubs did good business. In 2003 the village as a whole was finally settled in Pembrokeshire.

2. Poppit Sands

Poppit is one of Pembrokeshire's most popular beaches, good sand backed by sand dunes. Safe bathing inshore in the centre of the beach or where lifeguards indicate. The entrance to the river Teifi can be hazardous for vessels entering the estuary at certain states of the tide, and the estuary bar, a shifting sandbank, is known locally as the Cardigan bar. Cardigan's lifeboat station is at Poppit, equipped with two inshore lifeboats suitable for both the estuary and the rocky cliffs of the coast. The Teifi rises at Teifi Pools, on the Cambrian Mountains in mid Wales, running down to the sea through gorges and flat marshy areas. Cardigan island is a nature reserve in the hands of the

Poppit Sands

Wildlife Trust of South and West Wales, home to seabirds and grazed by a herd of soay sheep. Restricted access. Cardigan Bay is home to one of the very few resident Atlantic bottlenose dolphin pods in the UK; the local beaches and boats can provide good siting opportunities.

Start of walk, and the beginning (or end) of the Pembrokeshire Coast Path

Walk directions:

[-] denotes history note

1. Starting from the parking area at the Moorings walk towards St Dogmael's [1] to shortly pass the Ferry Inn on your left. There is a footpath signposted to the left through the Ferry Inn grounds, but this leads only to the jetty at the inn. Continue past the inn, to shortly bear left onto a signposted path – just past a house called *The Old Bakery*, currently painted pink.

2. Continue on the path above the river to reach the Green and the Teifi Netpool Inn. Follow the footpath around to the left of the Green. The Blessing Stone, in Welsh the *Carreg y Fendith*, where the Abbot blessed the fishing fleet, is signposted just off to the left before the picnic benches. The route onwards passes the standards on the left, wooden posts where the fishermen stretched out their nets, before descending to the river and the Pinog, where ships were built.

3. Stay on the path, ignoring the walkway leading up to the town car park, until it swings inland to meet the main road through St Dogmael's. The path can be flooded at high tides, if so cross the green in front of the Netpool Inn and continue across the playing field to the town car park. Bear left from there to rejoin the route.

4. Once at the main road bear right, continue past David Road, to turn left into Mill Street, opposite the White Hart. Continue past the working mill to

Stay on the path alongside the Teifi towards Cardigan until it swings inland

Teifi Netpool Inn

reach the abbey grounds and the Coach House. Go past the abbey ruins to reach a minor road. Bear right and continue ahead, ignoring roads leading off to the left.

5.	Shortly bear right onto a narrow path and passing a house named *Abbey Forge* on your left cross a footbridge and ascend to meet a minor road. Bear right. Continue uphill. Just before the road begins to go downhill bear sharp left onto a residential road at a No Through Road sign. Continue past the houses to reach a signposted footpath. Continue ahead – be aware of the sharp drop to your left. This is the cliff edge above Cwm Degwel (*Degwel valley*) ravine, the ravine created by glacial meltwater.

6. Continue to reach a waymarked post and bear right through a kissing gate into a field. Keep to the right edge to meet another gate giving access to a green lane. Stay ahead, ignoring a path leading off up steps on the right, to reach a field. Continue initially ahead and then bearing around to the right reach the farm track leading to Pencnwc farm on your right. Stay on the track to reach a minor road.

7. Bear left. Shortly bear right onto an open path – footpath sign by a telegraph pole here. Follow the path around to the left, and at a metal gate bear right to meet a farm gate. Go ahead across the field ahead, keeping to the right edge all the way round to meet a green lane. Follow the lane to reach the track leading to Bryncws farm. Bear right and follow the track to the road.

8.	Bear left and continue, leaving the road and taking a signposted bridleway leading off on the right at a bend in the road. Continue ahead to reach a crossroads of paths and tracks. Bear right onto another bridleway and follow this to reach a large open field. Go ahead on a

Bear right onto another bridleway

clear path as it descends to the farm of
Manian-fawr.

9. Bear left. Shortly leave the track and
bear right through a metal gate, almost
immediately bearing left. Continue, to
leave this path through a kissing gate on
the right, and follow this new path as it
bears around right, passing a caravan park

Follow the main road back alongside the Teifi to the start of the walk

on your left. Go ahead to reach the caravan park itself.

10. Continue ahead towards buildings. Bear right – there is a
big sign here pointing right stating Beach. Keeping the
buildings on your left follow the path onwards and around
to the left to reach a minor road. Bear right to reach the
beach and the road from Poppit Sands [2] to St Dogmael's.

11. Bear right onto the St Dogmael's road and follow it back
to the starting point. There are two small paths off to the
left running alongside the road before the Webley hotel is
reached. Short uphill section just after the Webley hotel,
otherwise on the level. There have been discussions on
introducing a new cyclepath/footpath between Poppit and
St Dogmael's, which would be a welcome addition.

Other information

Local producers' market held at the Coach House, the
visitor's centre and café to the abbey, every Tuesday 09.00
to 13.00. Adjacent to the abbey is Y Felin (*The Mill*), one of
Wales' last working mills, producing stone ground flour.
Café at Poppit Sands. St Dogmael's marks the start (or
finish) of the Pembrokeshire Coast Path, some 186
miles/299 kilometres in length, ending at Amroth on the
south coast. There is a plaque at the Moorings noting it's
start, as well as a carving of a mermaid, who advised one
local St Dogmael's fisherman of weather conditions after he
had released her after capture in his nets.

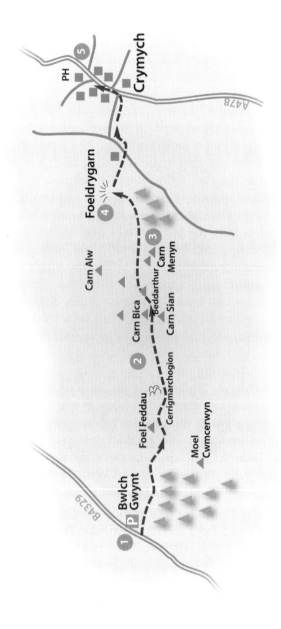

Walk 2
The Golden Road

Walk details

Approx distance:	*8.75 miles/14 kilometres*
Approx time:	*4½ hours*
O.S. Maps:	*1:25 000 North Pembrokeshire Outdoor Leisure 35*
Start:	*Bwlch Gwynt. As a linear route walk could alternatively start from Crymych.*
Access:	*Bwlch Gwynt can be found on the main road across the Preseli hills – the B4329. It is marked on the OS map.*
Parking:	*Rough parking possible at the start point.*
Going:	*Strenuous – mostly rough hill path (can get boggy), tarmac road at end.*

1. Bwlch Gwynt and the Golden Road

Bwlch Gwynt – the windy pass – stands at the highest point of the mountain road from north to south Pembrokeshire, and is a popular and convenient starting point for exploration of the Preseli hills. The route follows part of the Golden Road across the Preselis to the great Bronze Age cairn of Foel Drygarn. The description golden refers to the route's use during the Bronze Age as a trade route and trackway from Wessex in south-west England, to Whitesands Bay, near St David's, and Ireland, where goods, possibly locally made Preseli stone axes, were traded for copper and gold from the Wicklow hills. The track has had many names – the Pilgrim's Way, the Roman Road, the Robbers' Road. It was also known as the Flemings' Way, for the simple reason that Flemish settlers brought into the county by colonising Normans found it safer to take to the tops, out of the way of ambushing Welsh. Thousands of

Bwlch Gwynt – starting point and parking area to left of photo

cattle, sheep and pigs, even geese, with their drovers, would have used the route, particularly with the coming of toll gates to the plains, stamping out a path across the hills. Nowadays the hills are common land, grazed by the mountain ponies and the sheep during the better weather.

2. Bwlch Gwynt to Carn Menyn

The Preseli hills as we see them today are the remnants of a mountain chain thrown up during the Caledonian orogeny of four hundred million years ago – a mountain range that stretched from Britain to Scandinavia. The high cairns are made of harder igneous rock than the softer surrounding sedimentary and metamorphic rocks. Carn Bica, a typical Preseli cairn, may once have been used as a Bronze Age burial mound, but the stones have been much disturbed. Just below, to the right, is Beddarthur, the grave of King Arthur (one of many), the small stones delineating a grave of suitable size for so large a hero – however originally this may have been a Neolithic burial mound. At Carn Sian, Jane's Cairn, there is said to have been a chapel at some time in it's history, though no ruins survive. There is a plaque near Carn Sian, unveiled in 1984, in memory of a Liberator which crashed here in September 1944, killing five of the nine man crew. Grid reference OS 127322.

To the north east of Carn Bica, sited on Preseli's northern slope and off the route of the main walk, is Carn Alw, which has evidence of an Iron Age hillfort dating from

En route to Carn Menyn

the late first millennium BC. Utilising outcropping rock within it's rampart it's most distinctive feature is a *chevaux de frise* on it's west side. Rare in Britain a *chevaux de frise* is a defensive device whereby small stones are set upright in the ground by a defensive weakness. Here there are thousands of small stones up to a metre in height set in an arc of three separate bands around the entrance. Lack of evidence for habitation has led to speculation that the site may have been a base for summer upland grazing or as a refuge in case of attack. There is evidence of houses and cleared fields in the vicinity of Carn Alw, and there would have been permanent settlements to the north on lower ground. There may have been an earlier Bronze Age agricultural settlement to the south. Carn Alw is also unusual in that it is made of rhyolite, unlike the other outcrops in the eastern area of the Preselis which are of dolerite.

3. Carn Menyn

Carn Menyn, or Carn Meini, has lain claim to fame as the source for the bluestones of Stonehenge. It was in the early 1920s that the geologist H H Thomas claimed that many of the bluestones from the inner circle came from Carn Menyn. From this discovery grew the theory that Neolithic peoples transported over eighty stones, with a weight of over 250 tons, from one sacred site on the Preselis to another at Stonehenge, a distance of approximately 180 miles/290 kilometres. In the 1950s the BBC proved that such a feat was possible, using river and land transport. This popular theory is countered by the suggestion that the Irish Sea glacier, which at least once in it's history spread as far as Somerset and Avon, transported the stones there in their icy progress, and that when Stonehenge was built these stones were chosen as the most suitable. A medieval theory had Merlin as the magical agent, moving the stones with their healing properties from the so called Giant's Dance in Ireland when all others had failed to move them, and re-erecting them on their present site with the help of a giant. Recent excavations at Stonehenge in 2008 have led to the idea that fifty six bluestones formed a ring 285 feet/87 metres across as early as 3000 BC, thus making this the earliest stone structure known. These stones were then moved to the inner circle in 2300 BC. A further research, this time on the Preseli hills, has indicated that the bluestones, or at least some of them, came from nearby Carn Goedog and Craig Rhosyfelin, rather than Carn Menyn. There is at Carn Menyn a flat slab, cut as if ready for transport, and known as the altar stone; this may be all that is left of a small Neolithic burial chamber. No doubt many of the rocks owe their shape to shattering by frost, when the ground was frozen solid during the Ice Age. In April 1989 a bluestone pillar from here was flown down by helicopter

Carn Menyn skyline

En route to Foeldrygarn

and set up at Rhos Fach, on the minor road leading out from Mynachlog Ddu, whilst a twin was flown on to Stonehenge to act as a marker for the origin of the bluestones.

4. Foeldrygarn

Foeldrygarn, the hill of the three cairns, is the most spectacular of the Bronze Age cairns that dot the Preseli hills. It's siting, as with other Preseli Bronze Age cairns, is probably associated with the hill's use as trackway. Unlike Neolithic burial mounds, whose structure allowed for multiple burials, the Bronze Age cairns were built for a single occupant. It's strategic position proved ideal to later Iron Age people who built a large hillfort, incorporating the burial mounds within it. It had three defended enclosures. There is evidence of occupation from the first millennium BC to early first millennium AD, with indication of seventy seven platforms in the main inner enclosure, sixty three in the middle, and a further number in the annexe and outer area. Occupation would likely have been spread over different time periods. Gaps in the remaining walls may well be the original entrances.

5. Crymych

Originally a collection point for cattle droves Crymych in the early 1800s was just a few farms and houses then known as Iet y Bwlch (gate of the pass). The name by which the town and inn became known is an old one dating back to the 1460s, though it has had a number of spellings. One translation of it in it's present spelling is *crym*, meaning hunched up, and *ych* ox. The development of the town began with the arrival of the *Cardi Bach* railway (officially the Whitland and Taf Vale Railway) in July 1874. Begun in Whitland in November 1870 the 27½ mile long railway finally reached it's destination at Cardigan in September 1886. Originally constructed to carry local slate and lead ore it was agricultural products that proved it's mainstay. Market and mart grew rapidly, and new businesses and trades moved into the village. By the late 1880s the number of annual fairs had increased to twelve, including hiring fairs. Many of Crymych's new buildings added verandas for customers to tie up their horses, giving it the appearance of an Australian or Wild West country town; locally it became known as *Cowboy Town*. The railway closed in 1963, it's route still traceable in places. The town is still an important agricultural centre for the area, as it is culturally and educationally – the main comprehensive school for the Preseli area opened in the town in 1958, and *Ysgol Y Preseli* has been designated a bilingual school since 1991, science and English are taught predominantly through the medium of English, other subjects through the medium of Welsh.

Walk directions: [-] indicates history note

1. Starting from Bwlch Gwynt [1] take the obvious path heading out across the hills, keeping initially a fence, and then Pantmaenog Forest, to your right. Where the forestry ends there is access right up to open moorland and on to Preseli's highest point, Foel Cwmcerwyn. The Golden Road itself continues straight ahead, diverting to include Foel Cwmcerwyn will add well over a mile/1½ kilometres to the walk.

2. Continue on the Golden Road to Foel Feddau and it's Bronze Age cairn, and through the broken rocks of Cerrigmarchogion (*the rocks of the knights*). Continuing on the route is crossed by the deeply rutted tracks of the old north to south drover's road. Utilising the dip in the ridge the track led south from Eglwyswrw to Mynachlog Ddu and Maenclochog.

3. Continue on the clearly defined track to Carn Bica and

Beddarthur [2], and follow it on to Carn Menyn [3]. From Carn Menyn follow the path as it skirts the forestry plantation on the right.

Follow the path as it skirts the forestry

There are paths on the left en route which will lead up to the summit of Foeldrygarn [4], an easy one leads off left just after the forestry ends.

4. From Foeldrygarn descend to far corner where it abuts farmland and reach gate and stile. Cross and either continue on the track ahead,

Descend to the far corner

or bear left and then right on another track, to reach a minor road. Bear left and follow the road as it bends right and continue to reach the T junction with the A487. Bear left and continue on into Crymych [5].

Other information
All facilities available in Crymych.

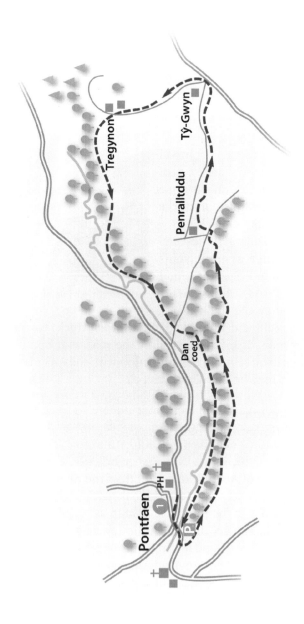

Walk 3
Pontfaen and the Gwaun Valley

Walk details

Approx distance: *5.5 miles/8.75 kilometres*

Approx time: *3 hours*

O.S. Maps: *1:25 000 North Pembrokeshire Outdoor Leisure 35*

Start: *The Dyffryn Arms in Pontfaen.*

Access: *Pontfaen is on the minor road running through the Gwaun valley – access from the B4313 from Fishguard, or from Dinas or Newport.*

Parking: *Parking at the side of the road opposite the Dyffryn. Also small parking bay on the left as you go uphill in the direction of the Maenclochog to Fishguard minor road – the bay is en route, just after leaving Pontfaen.*

Going: *Moderate – woodland paths, farm road.*

1. Pontfaen and the Gwaun valley

The delightful Gwaun valley (*gwaun* is Welsh for moor) was formed as a sub glacial meltwater channel of the formidable Irish Sea glacier. Rising on the slopes of Foel Eryr in the Preseli hills the river Gwaun runs for 8½ miles/14 kilometres down to Lower Fishguard, hence Fishguard's Welsh name of Abergwaun – mouth of the river Gwaun. It's slopes are densely wooded with oak, with alder and willow clinging close to the river. The Gwaun valley, along with the Daugleddau estuary, is one of the few remaining areas of semi-natural woodland left in Pembrokeshire, and is an area of rare beauty, it's river meandering on it's course past small farms and the occasional isolated settlement. The dippers and grey wagtails that frequent the hidden rock pools and the river make a fine contrast with the wild moorland pipits,

Pontfaen and the Gwaun valley

larks and buzzards. The valley's steep slopes have helped to keep communities and the natural landscape apart from the rest of the county, and preserve local traditions and individuality. When the new Gregorian calendar replaced the Julian calendar in 1752 local tradition ignored it. The Gwaun valley has the distinction of sharing with Lerwick in the Shetland Islands a New Year's Day of January 13th. The tradition of celebrating on January 13th persisted in the valley, many farmhouses hosting a party on *Hen Galan* (Old New Year's Day) with home brewed beer. Pontfaen (literally *Stone Bridge*) is typical of the small settlements that dot the valley. It's church, in ruins by 1861, was rescued from dereliction by the Arden family of Pontfaen House – it's nave and chancel probably date from circa 1200. There are 9th century memorial stones in the churchyard. The church is dedicated to the 6th century St Brynach, who lived for a while as a hermit on nearby Carn Ingli, the Rock of Angels.

Walk directions: [-] indicates history note
1. Starting from the Dyffryn Arms in Pontfaen [1] walk the short distance to the crossroads and bear left uphill in the direction of the Maenclochog to Fishguard minor road. Continue past the small parking area on the left as this will be the end point of the walk to reach another path leading off left by a telegraph pole – there is a Public Footpath sign on the pole. Pontfaen's church, signposted, is almost directly ahead on the right; worth a visit.

2. Continue ahead on the path through the wood, passing two paths leading off to the left, one fairly soon after entering the path, the other after approximately a mile/1½ kilometres. Continue to reach a signposted choice of

Pontfaen church

paths. Bear left over a footbridge and ascending steps reach a signposted bridleway. Bear right.

3. After a short distance the track breaks in two. Bear left to reach Penralltddu. Follow the waymarks past the barns and crossing the farmyard follow the track leading on to a minor road. Just before the minor road, at Ty-gwyn, bear left onto the track leading to Tregynon.

4. Once at Tregynon follow the waymarked path through the grounds, keeping the pond on your right. Ignore the path leading off to the right by the pond to continue ahead and left to re-enter the Gwaun valley woodland. Follow the path as it descends to meet a level path by a three way signpost. Bear left and continue ahead ignoring the turning to Sychbant en route to reach a track at Dan Coed.

5. Follow the route ahead over a footbridge and continue on the path as it ascends around the back of Dan Coed. Stay ahead, ignoring paths leading off to the left uphill, to reach the small parking area

Follow the path as it descends

Tregynon

Cwmgwaun Brewery

passed at the beginning of the walk. Bear right to return to the Dyffryn Arms.

Other information

Continuing the tradition of brewing in the valley is the microbrewery of the Gwaun Valley Brewery – it's ales on sale in the county. Situated on the Maenclochog Fishguard road, visitors welcome. Penlan Uchaf gardens and café, on the road from Pontfaen through the valley in the direction of Newport, open early spring to late autumn. Sychbant picnic site and toilets on the left, just before Penlan Uchaf.

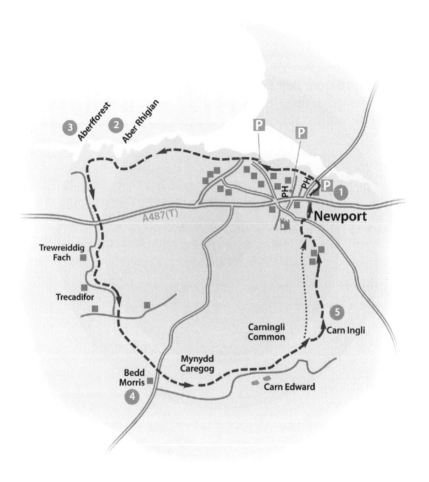

Walk 4
Newport and Carn Ingli

Walk details

Approx distance:	*9 miles/14.5 kilometres*
Approx time:	*4½ hours*
O.S. Maps:	*1:25 000 North Pembrokeshire Outdoor Leisure 35*
Start:	*The crossroads in the centre of Newport, ie the junction between Long St, Market St, Bridge St and East St.*
Access:	*Newport is on the A487 between Fishguard and Cardigan. Buses 405 The Poppit Rocket daily during summer May to September, less frequently during Winter; 412 Cardigan – Fishguard – Haverfordwest.*
Parking:	*Town car park in Long Street opposite the National Park Information Centre, and free down on the Parrog. Free parking by Newport bridge.*
Going:	*Strenuous – river, coastal and hill paths.*

1. Newport

The earliest man made structure remaining in the Newport town area is the Neolithic burial chamber of Carreg Coetan Arthur. Dated to 3500BC excavations in 1979 and 1980 showed that it had been surrounded and partially covered by a circular cairn of subsoil. Ploughing has built up a high level of soil around the uprights; the original structure would have originally appeared much

Carreg Coetan Arthur

27

The Parrog, Newport

taller. It's capstone now rests on two of it's original four sidestones. One of a number of such structures within the Newport and Nevern area it would have served the original farming community here who would have made a living through crop cultivation and animal husbandry, as well as river and coastal fishing, the river Nyfer which has it's outlet at Newport is still noted for it's salmon and trout. It's present name is one of many early structures to be associated with Arthur; in this case he used the stones (*carreg*) of the chamber to play *coetan* or quoits. Finds at the site include an axe fragment, flint knives and scrapers, and pottery fragments from probable cremation urns as charcoal and pieces of cremated human bone were found with them. It is in comparatively good condition and is signposted and easily found amongst modern bungalows on the left of Feidr Pen-y-Bont, the road leading down to Newport's late 19th century bridge across the Nyfer.

Settlement continued through the Iron Age and the early medieval period – there is a possible Iron Age fort or defensive harbour, Yr Hen Castell, (marked as *Enclosure* on the OS map), by the tennis courts on the left of the walk route shortly after leaving Newport bridge, but Newport's development as a town had to wait until the building of it's castle by the Norman William fitz Martin who had been driven out of his castle at Nevern by his father in law, the Lord Rhys, in 1191. The town that grew up in it's shadow was incorporated and given the name of *Novus Burgus*, New Town, or port. Fitz Martin also established St Mary's church, possibly on the site of an earlier 7th century church to St Curig. The castle was captured by the Welsh in 1215 and again in 1257, and may have been damaged in 1405 during the revolt of Owain Glyndŵr. By the 16th century it was in ruins, remaining so until the gatehouse and a flanking tower were converted into a private residence in 1859. It remains in private hands. The 13th century church retains it's original cruciform plan, but little of it's original structure remains apart from the 13th century stepped buttressed three storied tower. The church was enlarged in 1835, and then rebuilt in 1854, only to be restored in 1879. It's roof has been replaced. There is a fine Norman font, and close to it, set into the wall, a medieval holy water stoup. There is in the vestry a 14th century floriated cross-slab.

Newport became the capital of the Norman lordship of Cemaes and received privileges from William fitz Martin – the right to the annual appointment of mayor of Newport, with jurisdiction over a Court Leet, still exists. Despite a dangerous sand bar across the river mouth which hindered harbour development Newport had by the 16th century come to rival Fishguard in coastal trade. Out went slate to local ports and to Ireland, and slate stones to Bristol; herrings to France and Spain. For a while in the mid 16th century it was a woolen manufacturing centre with trade links with Bristol, which were to decline with an outbreak of plague, and a loss of trade to Fishguard. Alongside coastal trade and fishing went shipbuilding, and the town had a thriving shipyard by the end of the 18th century. The Parrog shipyards became noted; before 1830 for it's square rigged ships, after for it's schooners. In 1825 a new quay was built, trade increased, and the area, with it's shipyards, storehouses and coal yards became a bustle of activity. For a while, from 1800 to the 1830s, Newport was third only to

Milford and Lawrenny in the number of sailing vessels built and registered at the local ports of Milford, Pembroke and Cardigan. In came coal from Cardiff, slate from Gloucester, bricks from Cardigan, but with the development of land links the coastal trade inevitably declined, and the last vessel to call, the Agnes, landed her cargo of coal in September 1934. The quay walls survive, though in poor condition, and the last of the storehouses has become the Newport Boat Club. There is a double limekiln in good condition, with next to it the old limeburner's cottage. There is a slipway for launching dinghies, and dinghy sailing has become a popular sport here.

Newport has north Pembrokeshire's largest and most popular beach – Newport's Welsh name is after all Tredraeth, which can be translated as Beach Town. Lots of firm sand it is really two beaches, the larger and more popular Traeth Mawr (*big beach*) on the north side of the river, and the smaller Parrog Sands by the old harbour. It is possible to wade across the river at low tides. Traeth Mawr is backed by sand dunes, with parking allowed, at present, on the beach itself – there is also a car park. The estuary of

Traeth Mawr and Newport Boat Club

the river Nyfer offers a variety of habitats to local and visiting bird populations. As well as the trees alongside the river there are the mudflats, salt and freshwater marsh, and reed beds. As well as any number of mallard and gulls, recent visitors have included the little egret, often seen fishing to the right of the bridge by the reed bed, and a great number of geese. Needless to say the river and the area around the bridge are popular spots for local birdwatchers.

2. Aber Rhigian
One of Pembrokeshire's many small indented bays Aber Rhigian is backed by woodland, and close to and visible from the main A road to Newport, the unique circular 4th to early 3rd millennium BC Neolithic burial chamber of Cerrig y Gof (Rock of the Smith). Shingle and pebble backed the bay has sand at low tides.

Aber Rhigian

3. Aberfforest
Like Aber Rhigian another small unspoilt bay. Sandy at low tides, and popular with dinghy sailors. The limekiln at the head of the beach would have been in use in the days when local limestone, usually brought in direct by boat to beach, was burnt to provide lime for Pembrokeshire's acid soils.

4. Bedd Morris
The standing stone here traditionally marks the grave of Morris, or Morus, hence the Welsh name Bedd (*grave*) Morris. Morris himself was a notorious highwayman who

Aberfforest

View of the Preseli hills from Bedd Morris

Carn Ingli

took shelter amongst the rocks commanding the road down to Newport. Preferring bow and arrow as his method of attack, he trained his dog to retrieve any arrows that failed to meet their target. Incensed at his behaviour Morris was taken by the local populace, hanged, and buried beneath the stone. The stone itself is probably Bronze Age in origin, and would no doubt have indicated an important trade route. It has served for centuries as a boundary stone to Newport parish, and *Newport* can still be picked out, cut into the stone.

5. Carn Ingli

Once the core of a volcano the views from the present summit of Carn Ingli are quite superb. To the north are the rocks of Snowdonia, with the full panorama of the Preselis swinging around you to your right, whilst the splendid sea coast of Newport and Fishguard Bays lie etched below. One theory suggests that Carn Ingli was enclosed in the Neolithic period, another that the hillfort here was built by Iron Age settlers; either way the fort is spectacular. The still impressive single defensive wall in it's heyday may have been ten feet/three metres high. Traceable in the landscape are numerous hut circles and enclosures.

Possibly occupied until late Roman times it could have been home to some one hundred and fifty people. One notable Carn Ingli resident is said to have been the 6th century Irish St Brynach. A friend and contemporary of St David he founded a number of churches in the area, of which the church at Nevern, dating from 570, was the most important. Preferring to live the life of a hermit he chose Carn Ingli's splendid isolation as home. However St Brynach was no ordinary hermit. Not only was his coach driven by stags and his cows herded by a wolf, but he was also ministered to by a flight of angels. Quite possibly Carn Ingli takes it's name from the legend of St Brynach's life, and the Rock or Mount of Angels, Carn Engylion. In recent times stone was quarried from Carn Ingli's steep rock face

Carn Ingli Common and the Preseli hills

and transported via a cable railway to a crushing plant on the road below to the east. Two stone pillar blocks at the head of the incline are all that now remain of this brief industrial intrusion. Carn Ingli Common and Mynydd Caregog are typical of Pembrokeshire's upland scenery; gorse, bilberry and heather predominate, with on lower slopes occasional blocks of pine plantation. In late summer and autumn the yellows and purples of the gorse and heather turn the landscape into a glorious exhibition of colour.

Walk directions: [-] indicates history note
1. Starting from the crossroads in the centre of Newport [1] walk up the main A road in the direction of Cardigan to shortly bear left onto Feidr Pen-y-Bont (*Pen-y-Bont lane*), the road leading to Newport's golf course and Traeth Mawr

Starting from the crossroads

beach, and to Moylegrove. Passing Carreg Coetan Arthur burial chamber on the left (signposted), continue down to Newport's bridge.
2. Just before the bridge bear left onto a path leading alongside the Nyfer river and follow it to meet the

Parrog Road. Bear right and follow the route of the Coast Path, either along the foreshore, or if necessary follow the high tide alternative – route clearly marked; route goes up steps on the right just after Rock House's drive.

Alongside the Nyfer river

3. Continue on the Coast Path to the sheltered and pretty coves of Aber Rhigian [2] and Aberfforest [3]. From Aberfforest, just before reaching the beach, take the path leading off left by steps and leading away from the coast to reach the

Looking out over Newport Bay

road leading to Aberfforest houses and Marine, situated on the right. Follow the road left to reach the main A487.

4. Cross and bear right, and almost immediately bear left onto a marked bridleway. Currently there is a large sign for Havard Stables here. Continue inland, bearing left at Trewreiddig Fach and following the bridleway again shortly bear left and continue on the track to reach Trecadifor.

5. Pass the building on your right and follow a path uphill and where a choice of two paths are met bear left and follow an attractive green lane alongside a fence. Continue to reach a crossroads of paths. Continue uphill ahead and enter a field. Follow a clearly defined path through gorse and stay on it as it bears around to the left to emerge at a minor road. Bear right to reach the standing stone of Bedd Morris [4] and a small parking area on your left.

Path leading away from Carningli Common

6. Just to the left of the parking area is a clearly defined path leading out across Mynydd Caregog. Stay on this path, as it skirts fences to your right, and passing the rocks of Carn Edward en route finally reach Carn Ingli [**5**].

7. Choice to scramble up Carn Ingli's slopes and follow the path across the top through rocks, heather and bilberry, or stay on the flat and continue on a well defined path as it descends to fields. On meeting a field gate this route continues ahead, shortly bearing left, and at a concrete trackway it bears right, continuing downhill on a tarmac road, and passing the property of Castle Hill on the left.

8. If following the route across Carn Ingli descend and follow a clearly defined path down (this path is to the right of the flat path in front of Carn Ingli!) and where walled fields adjoin to the left and open country ends meet a fence and a gated track by a house on the right. Go through the gate and continue down, and at a crossroads of paths bear first left, and passing Bryn Eithin on your right meet a tarmac road. Castle Hill is on this road, uphill to the left. Bear right and continue downhill.

9. With both downhill routes meeting by Castle Hill simply descend. At College Square continue ahead and by St Mary's church either bear right and left, or continue ahead to reach Market Street, and then down, to reach the main A road through Newport. Bear right to regain the starting point.

Other information

All available in Newport. Public toilets on the Parrog. Golf course across the river. Tourist Information Centre in Long Street, opposite the car park; toilets at the car park.

Nyfer river at Newport Bridge

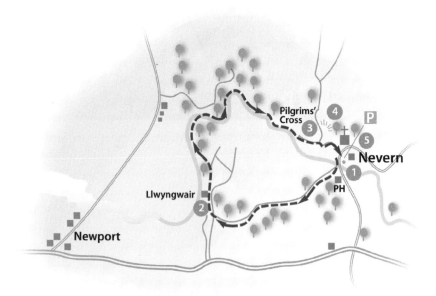

Walk 5
Nevern

Walk details

Approx distance:	*2.5 miles/4 kilometres*
Approx time:	*1¾ hours*
O.S. Maps:	*1:25 000 North Pembrokeshire Outdoor Leisure 35*
Start:	*Trewern Arms in Nevern.*
Access:	*Nevern is on the B4582, close to Newport, and a short distance from the A487 Newport to Cardigan road. Bus 412 Fishguard to Cardigan passes the turn to Nevern – the village is ½ mile/¾ kilometre from here.*
Parking:	*Limited parking in the village. Trewern Arms car park for patrons.*
Going:	*Easy – field and woodland paths, minor road.*

1. Nevern

One of the prettiest villages in Wales Nevern has had a rich and colourful history, it's layout following the pattern of Norman settlement. It's river, rising to the east of Crymych in the north-east of the county, is noted for it's fishing; sea and brown trout, and salmon. It's attractive bridge dates from the early 19th century. Nevern's old Welsh name is Nanhyfer, derived from an earlier Nant Nyfer, *nant* being the Welsh for brook.

Nevern (Nanhyfer)

39

2. Llwyngwair Manor

Llwyngwair Manor, now a hotel and caravan park, has a fine manor house. The country seat of the Bowens from 1540 until the family line recently died out the house has been much altered over the years, and is in effect an amalgam of styles from Tudor to Victorian. The Bowens were great patrons of the Methodists, John Wesley visited here, and William Williams Pantycelyn reputedly wrote what was to become one of the most popular of Welsh hymns here – possibly viewing Carn Ingli in one of it's bad moods he wrote *oe'r those gloomy hills of darkness, look my soul* ... Reflecting it's setting Llwyngwair translates as *hay grove*. Pontnewydd, *new bridge*, was built by the Bowens at a suitable crossing over the river Nyfer.

3. Pilgrims' Cross

Cut into the rock face here is the two foot high Pilgrims' Cross, with, below, a natural ledge where pilgrims may have knelt to supplicate the saints. Tradition has credited Nevern with being the last stage on the pilgrim route to St David's from St Dogmael's Abbey and North Wales. Certainly there were at one time eight pilgrim chapels of ease in Nevern parish, although by Elizabethan times they were in ruins. It is possible that this was the site of a healing well, Pistyll Brynach. Holy wells, springs, standing stones and Celtic church sites were much in favour as sources of bodily and/or spiritual strength. To the left of the cross, away from the road, are curious steps in the rock where the path begins a short ascent. No doubt cut by water there is a small graffiti cross cut into the stone. It is unlikely that pilgrims would have continued on the path to Newport, there are more direct routes, but pilgrimages were protracted affairs, with many side trips to different sites, and this would have been a wayside shrine, now almost unique.

4. Nevern Castle

More properly called Castell Nanhyfer, Nanhyfer being the original name for Nevern, the site has been subject to recent excavations. It is a fine example of a motte and bailey castle. One find dating from the 2008 excavation was a 12th century Nine Men's Morris board and counter. It was Robert fitz Martin, a Norman landowner from Devon, who took the old hundred of Cemais for himself to create a Norman enclave within Welsh territory, who built a double-motted castle here circa 1100, on the site of an earlier Welsh stronghold and probably an Iron Age settlement. His grandson William fitz Martin, who inherited the castle, had married Angharad, the daughter of the Lord Rhys, the native ruler of Deheubarth (south-west Wales), however this did not prevent his father in law from driving him out in 1191, giving the castle to his son Maelgwyn. Maelgwyn, together with a brother, later repaid his father by imprisoning him at Nevern for a brief time. William fitz Martin re-established Norman influence in the area in 1204, building himself a more substantial castle at Newport, with it's easy access to the sea. Nevern castle would then seem to have been abandoned by both Welsh and Norman.

5. Nevern church

St Brynach, to whom the present church is dedicated, established a religious settlement in the 6th century. A native of Ireland he had made his way here after pilgrimage to Rome, followed by sojourn in Brittany. He established a number of churches in the area, but seems to have preferred to live the life of a hermit on Carn Ingli, the *Rock of Angels*. A friend and contemporary of St David he is believed to have died on 7th April 570, St Brynach's day. Before they were driven out of Nevern the Normans had time to build a church on St Brynach's site, yet all that now remains is the 12th century tower. The rest of the church is late 14th century/early 15th century, and was much restored in 1864. The church and churchyard still, however, hold hidden treasure.

Nevern church

Embedded in the window sills of the south chapel, the Trewern-Henllys chapel, are two rare stone slabs found in 1906. The Maglocunus stone is a late 5th century or early 6th century memorial stone to Maglocunus, son (fili) of Clutorius. The inscriptions are in both Latin and ogham.

10th Century Cross Stone

Ogham is a script developed in Ireland by the late 5th century and is made up of a series of lines cut across the edge of the stone. Each letter of this Latin based alphabet is named from a tree or plant eg b from beith (birch). Next to it is the fine 10th century Cross Stone, with it's interlaced two cord cross. There is another bilingual memorial stone outside by the porch, to the 5th/6th century Welsh chieftain Vitalianus. However the pride of Nevern is the magnificent late 10th or early 11th century Great Cross – there are other superb examples at Carew and Penally in the south of the county. Inscribed on both sides only the meaning of that on the back of the cross can be guessed at – the letters DNS

Nevern Cross

an abbreviation of the Latin *Dominus*, Lord. In former days the first cuckoo of Spring is said to have sung from the head of the stone on St Brynach's day.

The fine avenue of English yews is believed to be six hundred years old – the second yew on the right from the churchyard entrance is famous for the almost continuous blood red sap that drips, some say, for a monk who was wrongly hung from the branches above. The line of Irish yews along the road were planted as a memorial to those who fought in the First World War. The mounting block by the entrance is one of only two left in Pembrokeshire, no doubt the occasional horse rider still makes use of it. The Nevern valley features in the medieval tales of the Mabinogion, for Twrch Trwyth, the wild boar, was pursued through the valley by Arthur and his knights to the Preseli hills. Nowadays the river is hunted only for salmon and sewin, returning from the sea at Newport Bay.

Walk directions: [-] indicates history note

1. Starting in Nevern [1] take the footpath leading across the field between the Trewern Arms and Nevern bridge – access next to a metal field gate. Signposted with walking man symbol. Cross the field to a wooded green lane and continue to reach the minor road by Llwyngwair Manor (now a hotel and caravan park) [2] – great views left en route of Carn Ingli's rock peak.

2. Bear right and continue past the old farm buildings. Where the road continues right to Llwyngwair Home farm continue ahead on a track, the route signposted just before a sign for Pontnewydd on the right. Continue to reach a footpath leading right, just past the bridge and the house on the left. Continue on this path, past a ruined cottage, to gain the riverside path.

3. Where the path meets a concrete roadway by a private house continue straight ahead across a footbridge, cross another private roadway and again go straight ahead to turn immediately right, waymarked. Cross the centre of the field to a stile to reach a path high above the river. Continue on this to reach another field.

4. Go ahead across the field, and keeping to the right field edge, reach a stile at the top right of the field. Cross onto the path leading past the Pilgrims' Cross [3] to reach the road into Nevern.

Nyfer river

5. At the road bear left uphill to the main castle site [4] entrance – field gate here. Either return back down this road, passing the access to the Pilgrims' Cross, or take the footpath leading downhill from the bailey, the cleared area in front of the old motte on which the old timber or stone tower would have stood – the path is not that easy to find but it is just past the ditch in front of the tower, descending through trees. If taking the road route where the road bears right continue ahead on a footpath by the side of a house to reach Nevern church [5] across an attractive stone footbridge. The route from the castle site leads down to this access path, just before the footbridge.

6. At the church continue along the footpath by the side of the church wall by a stream. From the church it is a short distance back to the starting point.

Back to the starting point

Other information

BT telephone, public toilets (by the community hall). Accommodation available in the village. Llwyngwair Manor is a popular caravan park. Pentre Ifan, possibly the finest Neolithic burial chamber in Britain, is two miles/three and a quarter kilometres to the south on a minor road; Castell Henllys, a recreation of an Iron Age fort, is two miles/three and a quarter kilometres to the north on the A487. Both are signposted.

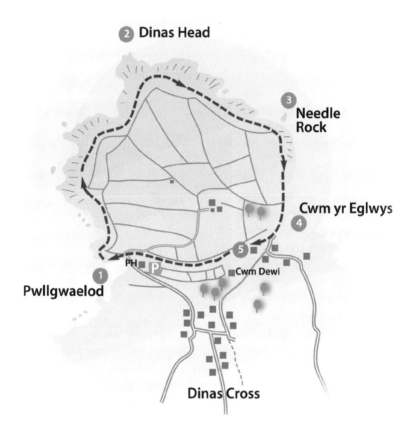

2 **Dinas Head**

3 **Needle Rock**

Cwm yr Eglwys

4

5

Cwm Dewi

PH P

1 **Pwllgwaelod**

Dinas Cross

Walk 6
Dinas Head

Walk details

Approx distance: *3 miles/4.75 kilometres*

Approx time: *1½ hours*

O.S. Maps: *1:25 000 North Pembrokeshire Outdoor Leisure 35*

Start: *Pwllgwaelod*

Access: *Pwllgwaelod is reached from the village of Dinas Cross, on the A487 Fishguard to Newport road. Bus 405 Fishguard to Cardigan (the Poppit Rocket) calls at Pwllgwaelod daily during it's summer timetable May to September, bus 412 Haverfordwest to Fishguard to Cardigan calls at Dinas Cross all year round.*

Parking: *Free parking at Pwllgwaelod. Parking also possible at Cwm-yr-Eglwys.*

Going: *Easy – coastal and inland paths.*

1. Pwllgwaelod

Pwllgwaelod, which can be translated as bottom pool, has always been popular, and can get crowded on hot summer days. Still popular with local fishermen the small car park at the head of the beach often doubles up as a boat park. The limekiln, a little way inland from the beach, would have produced lime for fertilising Dinas Island farm, and farms around Dinas Cross.

Pwllgwaelod

2. Dinas Head

Dinas Head, or rather Pen y Fan (*head of the peak*), stands at 466 feet/142 metres high. It's survival as a headland is due to the Silurian grits of which it is partly formed, harder rock than the surrounding softer Ordovician shales and sandstones which have fallen victim to the sea's adventuring. There are the ruins of a former coastguard lookout by the OS trig point. In addition to Newport Bay there are magnificent views south over Fishguard Bay to Garn Fawr and Strumble Head, and inland to Dinas Cross and the outlying hills of the Preseli range. From the headland there are good chances of seeing seals in the waters below, perhaps even a harbour porpoise or dolphin. Local tales tell of a fisherman who when he cast anchor off the headland received an unexpected visitor. One of the fairy folk, the Bendith y Mamau, who had their city under the sea here, climbed up the anchor rope and complained the anchor had gone through his roof. Dinas Island farm, some four hundred acres, was once an Elizabethan grange which provided game for the formerly splendid Pentre Ifan mansion, near Newport. Former holders have included the naturalist Ronald Lockley, founder of Britain's first bird observatory at Skokholm, who raised cattle, sheep, corn and early potatoes for a number of years and wrote of his time there in *Island Farmer* and *Golden Year*.

Pen Dinas headland

3. Needle Rock

The attraction here is Needle Rock, the great sea stack which provides a grand home for breeding guillemots and razorbills from April to July. With the clamour of breeding kittiwakes and gulls, jackdaws and fulmars this can be a noisy and entertaining place. There are usually a few young fulmars, hatched on the cliffs below, present until September, but most sea birds have by then left to overwinter at sea. Great views from here of Newport Bay, with Cardigan island and the great rock folds of Cemaes Head and Pen yr Afr in sight on clear days, with inland Carn Ingli and Newport, the castle and church tower just visible.

4. Cwm yr Eglwys

Cwm yr Eglwys (*valley of the church*), like it's close neighbour Pwllgwaelod, is one of the most popular beaches on the north coast, but unlike Pwllgwaelod with it's grey sand, has fine golden sand at low water. The 15th century church, of which only the western wall and belfry survive, was destroyed, along with low lying cottages and the quay, in a truly ferocious storm in October 1859 which wrecked shipping all around the Welsh coast. Of the 114 ships wrecked the worst was the *Royal Charter*, sunk off Anglesey with the loss of 459 lives. A new church was built on safer ground, inland at Bryn-henllan, in 1860. Like it's predecessor it was dedicated to the 6th century St Brynach. One of the many coastal trading ports Cwm yr Eglwys was, at least in the late 18th century, known

Cwm yr Eglwys

49

as Dinas Harbour. Sheltered as it is from the prevailing westerlies, the cove shows a marked difference in appearance to Pwllgwaelod. Trees and shrubs flourish here, adding their softer greens to the blues and greys of the sea and sky.

5. Cwm Dewi

Cwm Dewi is a pleasant marshy and wooded valley, popular with the local bird life, and watched over by the Dinas island rabbits and sheep. It was formed some 17,000 to 20,000 years ago as a meltwater channel for the glacier then blocking Newport Bay, making Dinas island truly an island – because of this Dinas Head often gets referred to as Dinas island. Later infills of boulder clay have helped form the valley as it is today.

Walk directions: [-] indicates history note

1. Starting from Pwllgwaelod [1] head up the road to the left of the pub, and bearing left join the coast path to reach Dinas Head [2] – don't follow the road inland to the farm!

2. A short distance after leaving the headland there is a choice of paths. The coastal route drops down off the ridge, giving a better view of Needle Rock [3], though in wet weather or after rain it can be muddy. The drier route continues along the ridge. Both routes join by Cwm-yr-Eglwys [4].

3. Once at Cwm-yr-Eglwys, keeping initially to the right of the car park, follow the valley path along Cwm Dewi [5] the 0.5 miles/0.75 kilometres back to Pwllgwaelod.

Coastal path after leaving Pwllgwaelod

Other information

Pwllgwaelod has a pub by the beach. Public toilets at Pwllgwaelod and Cwm-yr-Eglwys. Most other facilities are available in Dinas Cross, including garage and mini market and two more pubs.

Looking out over Newport Bay

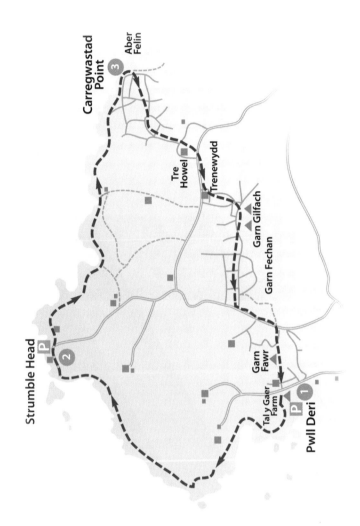

Walk 7
Pwll Deri, Strumble Head, Carregwastad Point and Garn Fawr

Walk details

Approx distance: *9 Miles/14.5 Kilometres*

Approx time: *4 hours*

O.S. Maps: *1:25 000 North Pembrokeshire Outdoor Leisure 35*

Start: *Pwll Deri. Strumble Head would make an alternative starting point, plenty of parking space available as at Pwll Deri.*

Access: *Pwll Deri is 5.5 miles/9 kilometres from Fishguard. Can also be reached from the south through St Nicholas. Bus 404 the Strumble Shuttle Fishguard to St David's stops at Strumble Head (Strumble Head junction in winter) and Trefasser Cross.*

Parking: *Parking bay at Pwll Deri.*

Please note: *May be treated as 2 separate walks if preferred, using the road to Strumble Head as a link path: Pwll Deri – Strumble Head – Garn Fawr – Pwll Deri 5.5 miles/9 kilometres, Strumble Head – Carregwastad Point – Tre Howel – Strumble Head 6 miles/9.5 kilometres.*

Going: *Strenuous – mainly coastal path, farm track and green lane.*

1. Pwll Deri

Pwll Deri, pool of the oak trees, is as attractive as the name suggests, with the sheer cliffs dropping down to the sealbright sea, and the rock headland striding down to St David's Head. Not many oak trees though, too windy for that! A popular place for those who like their scenery wild and dramatic. There is a memorial here to the Welsh poet

Pwll Deri

Dewi Emrys, who immortalised Pwll Deri in a poem written in the local dialect. The landscape to Strumble Head and beyond is one of igneous headlands, intercut with bays where the softer sedimentary rocks predominate. Dinas Mawr, as might be expected from it's strategic position, was once an Iron Age fort, protected on it's landward side by double banks. Trefasser is believed to be the birthplace of Bishop Asser, the 9th century friend, counsellor and chronicler of the Anglo-Saxon king of Wessex, Alfred the Great – he who burnt the cakes. Asser spent his youth studying at St David's monastic community, from where he was enlisted for service by Alfred, dividing his time from circa 885 onwards between the court and St David's. En route to Strumble Head, just before the derelict Ministry of Defence buildings, steps have been cut down to the beach of Porth Maenmelyn through a cleft dynamited out by a Mr Clark, one of the engineers who worked on Fishguard Harbour in 1908, and who lived in the house which is now the Youth Hostel. Just the kind of hidden and lonely place to be made use of by smugglers. Access to the beach has been guarded by a metal gate.

2. Strumble Head

Strumble Head is dominated by it's splendid lighthouse. Built by Trinity House in 1908 at the time Fishguard

Inside the lighthouse

Harbour was being built, it's location on Ynys Meicel was seen as ideal for guiding ships safely around to the new harbour. Nowadays the lighthouse is automatic, monitored from St Ann's Head light. Access is across a narrow footbridge, but no visitors allowed. Light visibility is good for over 31 nautical miles, it's booming foghorn audible for 5 nautical miles. Strumble Head is a noted location for bird and sea watchers, with spring and autumn bird migrations, and the early morning and late evening summer passage of Manx shearwaters skimming low over the water from their breeding sites on the Pembrokeshire islands to feeding sites in Cardigan Bay. An old Ministry of Defence building has been converted to provide basic shelter for sea watchers. The coastline here is a prime location for harbour porpoises.

Strumble Head lighthouse

3. Carregwastad Point

Carregwastad is famous as the site of the last invasion of Britain in February 1797. As part of the French wars against England and Austria a proposal was devised to conduct a war of privateers against the English, with landings on Irish and British soil to ferment anarchy and provide support for rebels. On 16 February 1797 an expedition of 1400 men, the Légion Noire under the command of an Irish-American with experience of fighting in the American War of Independence, a Colonel Tate, left Brittany, bound for either Bristol or South Wales. Unable to land at Bristol the expedition of four ships sailed on, rounding St David's Head on Wednesday 22nd February 1797. Recognised, and forced out of Fishguard Bay by a single shot from Fishguard fort, it was decided to take advantage of the calm weather and moonlit night, and accordingly the men and stores were landed at the steep cliffs of Carregwastad Point.

As planned the ships returned to France, while Colonel Tate set up his headquarters at Tre Howel farm. Transport and food being the requirement the men, mainly grenadiers and ex-convicts, set out to scour Pencaer peninsula. January 1797 had seen a Portuguese coaster wrecked off the coast, and the majority of farms in the area had fine Portuguese wine in addition to cattle, pigs, poultry and sheep. Here the invasion started to go wrong, and the motley assortment of troops, making no attempt at concealment, decided to liberate the wine instead of the local populace. As a result several hundred of the invasion force deserted camp en masse. By this time panic was spreading throughout the area, with both locals and French killed and injured.

Fortunately the heroes of the hour were close at hand in the shape of Lord Cawdor of Stackpole and his Castlemartin Yeomanry, who, on hearing of the invasion, had marched north, collecting all able bodied men en route. They arrived at Fishguard early in the evening of the 23rd, ready to face the French, who were now deployed on the cliffs overlooking Goodwick. The night being particularly dark, the drums were sounded for recall, and Lord Cawdor's men retreated. The French, thinking the drums sounded the advance, also retreated, firing as they went. Stalemate.

Lord Cawdor's men in their blue uniforms had already been sighted by the French before they reached Fishguard, yet it is said the French also saw, silhouetted against the gun metal sky, another force dressed in red. These are believed to have been the local women who had gathered on the hills in their red cloaks, to act as spectators or soldiers as necessary. Cometh the hour, cometh the woman, and one Jemima Nicholas of Fishguard, not content to be a spectator, marched into battle with a pitchfork, rounded up twelve Frenchmen, and marched them off to Fishguard guardhouse.

Memorial stone at Carregwastad Point, 1897 still just discernable

The combination of events, desertions and dissatisfied officers led Tate, by late on the Thursday evening, to sue for peace. Terms were agreed and the surrender signed on the morning of Friday 24th February 1797 at the Royal Oak in Fishguard – the table on which they signed is still there, with other memorabilia of events. The memorial stone was erected in 1897, in commemoration of the event.

The sheltered shingle beaches of Aber Felin bay are ideal for the local grey seals. Pupping takes place from September to December, with each female dropping a single pup, and the inaccessibility of the bay provides a safe and protected site. Good views north of the sloping flat top of Dinas Head, and on to Cemaes Head and Cardigan island.

Aber Felin

4. Garn Fawr

At 699 feet/213 metres Garn Fawr is the highest point on Pencaer peninsula. An early Iron Age fort is it's crowning glory, with at least three ramparts still traceable. Entrance would have been from the eastern, more accessible side. However the stones have been borrowed and moved around so much that the original layout is difficult to determine. There was a radar station here during World War Two, but now only the walls remain. Glorious views of the table top peninsula below, neatly divided up into pocket handkerchief

Pencaer peninsula from Garn Fawr

Stone cell

sized fields, with attendant white wall dwellings and farms. Inland the great Lion Rock of Treffgarne gorge turns away from the Preseli hills towards St Brides Bay and the islands. In Pwllderi holiday cottages courtyard is an early stone beehive hut, described variously as an early monk's cell, and, unkindly, as a prehistoric pigsty. It is to the left as you enter the courtyard from the heights of Garn Fawr. Just room enough to stand up in.

Walk directions: [-] indicates history note

1. From Pwll Deri [**1**] join the Coast Path and continue the 3 miles/5 kilometres or so to Strumble Head [**2**].

2. From Strumble Head continue on the Coast Path to

Where the Coast Path goes left go ahead

Carregwastad Point [3]. This section is also just under 3 miles/ 5 kilometres; the neat whitewashed cottage of Penrhyn marking the halfway point.

3. From the monument on Carregwastad Point continue a short distance on the Coast Path, and where the Coast Path goes left go ahead on a footpath to reach a gate. Small hill in front of you.

4. From the gate bear right and then left and follow a clear path up the side of the hill through gorse to enter a field. Well waymarked. Keeping the fence to your left reach a stile.

5. Cross and join a farm track. Stay on this track to reach a farm gate and a choice of paths. Continue ahead and right, following the route through Tre Howel farm to reach the minor road to Strumble Head. Tre Howel acted as the French headquarters during the brief invasion of 1797.

6. Bear right and continue to Trenewydd. Turn left here, and go between the farmhouse and the barn to join a farm lane/bridleway leading uphill. Continue uphill to reach a T junction with another lane/path. Turn right, and continue, keeping the dry stone wall/hedge to your right. Garn Gilfach will now be above left.

7. Continue to reach a farm gate giving access to a green lane – the path well flanked by bluebells in season. Go ahead. Shortly before reaching a minor road there is the choice of following a footpath on the left (well signposted, and crossing a stone stile), taking you over Garn Fechan and on to reach a minor road opposite a small car park, or stay on the bridleway as it continues downhill to reach a minor road. If choosing the bridleway bear left at the road and continue uphill on the minor road to reach the small car park, on the right.

8. Turn right onto the footpath by the car park and continue uphill to Garn Fawr [4]. From Garn Fawr descend straight down through Tal Y Gaer farm/Pwllderi holiday cottages to Pwll Deri and the starting point.

Other information

Parking also possible at Strumble Head, and at the small car park on the landward side of Garn Fawr. Youth hostel and camping site at Pwll Deri, BT telephone at Trefasser. No other facilities.

Footpath access to Garn Fechan

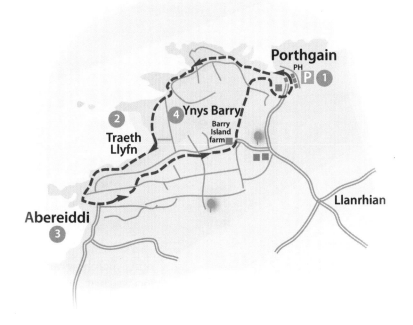

Walk 8
Porthgain and Abereiddi

Walk details

Approx distance:	*3.5 miles/5 kilometres*
Approx time:	*2 hours*
O.S. Maps:	*1:25 000 North Pembrokeshire Outdoor Leisure 35*
Start:	*Porthgain's car park, in front of the Sloop Inn.*
Access:	*Porthgain is situated on the coast roughly halfway between Fishguard and St David's. From the A487 at Croesgoch follow the minor road through Llanrhian. Bus 404 the Strumble Shuttle Fishguard to St David's calls at Porthgain, as does the 413 on schooldays.*
Parking:	*Spacious car park in Porthgain.*
Going:	*Easy – coastal path, field and farm track.*

1. Porthgain

Anyone visiting Porthgain for the first time will immediately be aware of the imposing ruins marching up the cliff face from the harbour. A visitor 160 years or so ago would have seen none of this, perhaps only a huddle of fishing boats drawn upon a different shoreline, for Porthgain's harbour owes it's present shape to man-made construction. Porthgain's geology has given the area an identity and industrial history unique in Pembrokeshire. The metamorphosed shale here gave slate for flooring and roofing, the clay was used for brick making, and the volcanic dolerite rock provided roadstone for Britain's developing roads. Porthgain's industrial revolution started in 1837 when George Le Hunte, the local landowner, granted a lease to a local company to extract flags, slates and stones. However it was a London consortium, Barclay & Company,

Porthgain

who were granted other leases in 1840, who started the transformation. The first harbour was built, the first quarries were developed, and the first tramway joining nearby Abereiddi and it's slate quarry to Porthgain harbour was laid. Brick making had to wait until 1878, when, under the St Brides Slate & Slab Co., Porthgain's heavier than normal bricks began to find their way to places as far afield as Dublin and Bridgwater. By 1912, after several changes of ownership, there were three steam locomotives, plus traction engines and motor lorry, on site. One loco, the Charger, had seen service in the Jarrow shipyards, the others were the *Singapore*, and appropriately, as first engine, the *Porthgain*.

Maritime reminder at Porthgain

The slate and brick industries here fell into decline by the early 1900s, and crushed stone took on greater importance. Small pieces of blasted stone were hauled up the Jerusalem Road from Porthgain's quarry and crushed into sizes from 0.25 to 2.5 inches and stored in the hoppers. They were then exported by company ship or road. By

64

1931 fortunes declined, and in August of that year business closed. There are still extensive ruins worth exploration. The present Harbour Lights gallery was the former company offices, and Ty Mawr, the recently restored building adjacent to the green, was connected with brick making. The stone chutes and hoppers dominate the harbour, and the old tunnel cut through to Porthgain's slate quarry can be easily picked out. On the cliffs above are the ruins of the former quarrymen's cottages, and the loco shed, weighbridge and water tower still partially stand. The extensive quarry and ruined smithy can be explored from the *Jerusalem Road*. The village is now in local ownership, with the harbour, quarries and cliff land the responsibility of the National Park.

2. Traeth Llyfn

Traeth Llyfn, translated as the smooth, or sleek beach, does have a fine sandy beach. Good for swimming, though there is a strong outgoing current, noticeably to the left. From the headlands around Traeth Llyfn the rock outcrops of Carn Llidi and Pen Beri appear as truly imposing mountains dominating St David's Head. St Finbar is said to have sailed from here to found the city of Cork, while Columba sailed en route to Iona.

Traeth Llyfn

3. Abereiddi

The slate quarry here at Abereiddi was part and parcel of Porthgain's industrial enterprise. The poor harbour, vessels of only twenty to thirty tons could load from the quarry slip, meant that the construction of a tramway to Porthgain harbour was essential. In length just under two miles, trains, consisting of usually two or three wagons, were hauled by two horses to the Slate Yard near Barry Island farm for storage, before being shipped out. The quarry was at it's busiest from circa 1850 to 1904, with exports of Abereiddi and Porthgain slate to Bristol Channel and English Channel ports. The ruins of the engine house, the dressing sheds, and the quarrymen's cottages known as The Row, are still evident. Sometime after quarrying had ceased the connecting walls leading from the old engine house around to the dressing sheds were blasted away, resulting in a small harbour, well known locally as *The Blue Lagoon* – the water truly is blue! The bay is famous in geological circles for the fossil graptolites found in it's Ordovician slates when split. A first was recorded here with the discovery of a previously unknown example of these plant-like animals. There is a possibly 18th century observation tower on Trwyn Castell head overlooking Abereiddi bay. A curious building, there is even a fireplace inside should you need to warm up. Like many remote headlands on the Pembrokeshire coast Trwyn Castell would have been home to Iron Age settlers.

The Blue Lagoon, with the agreement of the National Trust, has been the UK stop of the Red Bull Cliff Diving World Series. Diving from a

The Blue Lagoon, Abereiddi

27

Approaching Abereiddi, Trwyn Castell, and the observation tower

metre high board athletes have three seconds to execute acrobatic dives, reaching speeds of 85kph. Quite a sight.

4. Ynys Barry (*Barry island*)

Barry island takes it's name from a geological feature of the landscape, hinted at by the narrow valley along which the tramway from Abereiddi ran. As the Ice Age came to an end the Irish Sea ice melted, and a sub glacial meltwater channel was formed which ran down to Abereiddi Bay and provided temporary island status. Dinas island (more properly Dinas Head), near Newport, owes it's landscape charter to similar action.

Walk directions: [-] indicates history note

1. From the car park in Porthgain [**1**] walk down to the harbour to pass the old stone chutes. By the stone building (the former Pilot House) climb the steps to reach the headland. To the right, on the headland, there is a stone pillar, matched by another on the opposite side of the harbour. These mark the harbour entrance.

2. Continue ahead. After a short distance the path breaks in two. Keep to the left hand path – the right, known as the *Jerusalem Road*, leads downhill to the old quarry and the ruins of the smithy. Keep to the level path, passing to the left above the quarry, and follow the Coast Path to Traeth

Abereiddi – following winter storms a new shoreline is developing, with new sea defences planned

Llyfn [2]. Metal steps lead down to this popular beach.

3.　　Continue on the Coast Path as it bears right around the beach headland, and follow it on to Abereiddi [3] – bear right on a level path before heading down to the beach to reach the Blue Lagoon. Once at Abereiddi proper head inland from the beach, past the ruined quarrymen's cottages, to reach a path by the public toilets.

4.　　Cross into the field ahead. Keep to the top of the slope and continue ahead to reach a wooden stile. Cross and keeping to the right field edge continue to a field gate. Ignore the stile in front of you – this leads back to the coast – and instead continue right on a farm track.

5. Follow the farm track across Ynys Barry [4] to Barry Island farm and bear left just after the farm buildings on a signposted track. Keeping to the right and then left of fields reach a path bearing right back to Porthgain and the starting point – left would take you back to the headland above the harbour.

Back to Porthgain

Other information
Parking is also possible at Abereiddi, where there are public toilets, emergency telephone, and seasonal ice cream van. Bistro and the Sloop Inn in Porthgain, as well as two art galleries, public telephone and toilets.

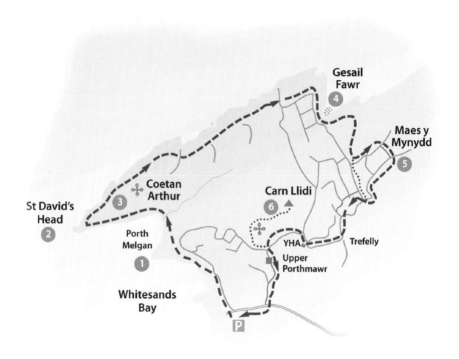

Gesail
Fawr
4

Maes y
Mynydd

5

St David's
Head
2

Coetan
Arthur
3

Carn Llidi
6

Porth
Melgan
1

YHA

Trefelly

Upper
Porthmawr

Whitesands
Bay

P

Walk 9
Whitesands Bay and St David's Head

Walk details

Approx distance:	*5 miles/8 kilometres*
Approx time:	*3 hours*
O.S. Maps:	*1:25 000 North Pembrokeshire Outdoor Leisure 35*
Start:	*Coast Path at Whitesands Bay car park.*
Access:	*Whitesands Bay is reached on the B4583 from St David's. Seasonal Celtic Coaster 403 bus service from St David's.*
Parking:	*Whitesands Bay car park – seasonal charge.*
Going:	*Moderate – coastal path, field and track.*

1. Whitesands Bay

The Welsh name Traeth Mawr means Great Beach. It's golden sands make it a popular place in summer. Popular also with surfers and canoeists all year round – the bay is one of the best surfing beaches in Wales. Boats leave from here for trips around Ramsey island in the high season. At exceptionally low tides there are the remains of a prehistoric forest, as well as those of the wreck of the paddle tug *Guiding Star*, aground in 1882. Porth Melgan, by St David's Head, provides a less hectic, but equally rewarding summer beach. Popular fiction has gifted Cornwall with it's fair share of coastal smuggling. However Cornwall was not alone. An 1807 account notes the arrest of a smuggling vessel in Whitesands Bay by the coastguard cutter *Hope*. The crew had been in the process of transferring a cargo of spirits into smaller casks. The empty casks would have been brought out from local shores, quite possibly from the comparative safety of Ramsey island. Surely an indication of a booming local trade!

Whitesands Bay

During the 5th and 6th centuries Wales experienced the full force of the monastic movement – truly the Age of the Saints. St David, a Pembrokeshire man and Wales' patron saint, established his church and monastery in the nearby city in around 550. One aspect of this monastic movement was the continual travelling of both saints and disciples on missionary journeys between not only the emergent Celtic nations, but also to places as far afield as Iceland. It was customary to pray for delivery from danger prior to sea journeys, and similarly to give thanks after the journey, using wherever possible wide sandy beaches for the landing. Chapels, dedicated to the saints, began to dot the Celtic coastline. St Patrick, Ireland's patron saint, reputedly sailed from Whitesands Bay to Ireland, and the chapel built on the site was dedicated to him. Nothing now remains but the site, however the area was excavated in the 1920s and the skeleton of a young man found. The site is to the left of the path, almost immediately after leaving the car park at the beginning of the walk.

2. St David's Head

There is a fine Iron Age promontory fort on St David's Head, protected by the remnants of the *Clawdd Y Milwyr* – the Warrior's Dyke. The original inner rampart would have been 15ft/4.5m high by 12ft/3.5m thick at the base, with two smaller walls and three ditches. The entrance would have been across a causeway and through a 7ft/2m wide passageway. Dated to 100 AD the site may have developed over two different periods. Within the settlement, at the foot of a rock outcrop, clearly visible are eight hut circles, the remains of circular stone houses which would have been thatched with bracken, rushes or grass. These provided the living quarters. There are the remains of a stone wall stretching obliquely across the headland from Porth Llong a quarter of a mile/half a kilometre away, defining a wider settlement area. Probably making their living by mixed farming and stock breeding the Iron Age settlers may have used this area for stock as well as for living. The Porth Melgan valley and the western slopes of Carn Llidi may have been used as fields. Evidence of stone field boundaries are there on the valley slopes, but are probably of a later date. Worthy of exploration the area is now haunted only by the cries of gulls, oystercatchers, and the local choughs.

Carn Llidi from St David's Head

3. Coetan Arthur

Prior to the arrival of Iron Age settlers the area was occupied by Neolithic immigrants. Arriving from 3,000 BC onwards they lived by crop raising and animal herding. Little remains of their flimsy houses, what have survived are the cromlechau, the stone burial chambers. Originally covered by earth or stones, with the upright pillars infilled with dry stone walling, only their stone structures survive. Coetan Arthur – Arthur's quoit – has been dated to circa 3,000 BC. There are the remains of two other burial chambers on the western slope of Carn Llidi, one with it's capstone dislodged. Later peoples, not knowing the history of prehistoric monuments, came to associate them with the heroes of legend; Arthur, Samson and the Devil strode the landscape, and the Druids made human sacrifice on the capstones.

4. Gesail Fawr

The near inaccessibility of Gesail Fawr is typical of the indented North Pembrokeshire coastline and the Pembrokeshire islands. However this inaccessibility is good news for the grey seals. These remote beaches, including Gesail Fawr, are the scene of frenetic activity when in autumn the females come ashore to drop a single pup. The male will protect a harem of five to ten females. Diving seals normally stay under water for five minutes or so, however a

Coetan Arthur

dive can last for up to twenty minutes. So if you are waiting for a seal to re-surface you may have a long wait!

5. Maes y Mynydd

The remains at Maes y Mynydd (*the mountain field*) are those of a deserted village. First recorded in 1829 a tithe map of 1840 indicates six or seven houses, though at one time there may have been as many as thirteen. Living was mainly maritime based. Abandoned in the early 20th century local tradition has associated the village with the Quakers.

6. Carn Llidi

It is well worth taking time out for the ascent of Carn Llidi – easily climbed from it's western side. The views from the summit can be breathtaking. From the summit the flatness of the landscape becomes obvious. The plateau would have been formed as a result of constant wave action at a time when the land was beneath the sea. Only the harder igneous outcrops such as Carn Llidi would have resisted the wave erosion. The track leading to the lesser summit was built during World War One and led to a hydrophone station which detected enemy submarines. In World War Two the site was extended to become a radar station with scanners on Carn Llidi. Only the base of the buildings now remain. The two cromlechau mentioned under Coetan Arthur are to the right of the track, just below the lesser summit.

Carn Llidi and Maes y Mynydd

Walk directions: [-] indicates history note

1. From Whitesands Bay [**1**] car park join the Coast Path through the gap in the stone wall, to the right of the telephone kiosk.

2. Follow the Coast Path uphill, passing the site of St Patrick's chapel on your left, and continue on to Porth Melgan and St David's Head [**2**] 1 mile/1.5 kilometres away.

3. From St David's Head fork left, passing Coetan Arthur on your right [**3**], and continue for a mile/1.5 kilometres to reach a gate set into a stone wall.

4. Continue on the Coast Path to pass above Gesail Fawr [**4**] and reach another gate. Go through and passing rocks above right shortly leave the Coast Path, bearing right and uphill. There is a footpath sign here, well waymarked.

5. Continue uphill on the path to reach a green lane. Do not enter, but instead bear left on a path, and keeping the stone wall to your right continue to reach the access lane to Maes y Mynydd [**5**].

6. At the end of the lane bear right and continue alongside the field boundary to reach farm gates to your right. Go through the gate to your left, and bearing around left reach another gate – great views of Ramsey and Skomer islands framing St Brides Bay!

Continue on the Coast Path to pass above Gesail Fawr

7. Bear diagonally left across the field to meet the farm lane leading to Trefelly.

8. Continue down the lane until just before the farm access gate cross right a stile leading into a field.

9. Cross two fields to reach the Youth Hostel. Turn right here and continue up a lane to a gate giving access on to the footpath skirting Carn Llidi [6] – a most imposing view!

10. Turn left and continue to meet the farm lane leading down to Upper Porthmawr. Turn left and follow the track through the farm and down to the road leading to Whitesands Bay.

Cross stiles to reach the Youth Hostel

11. Bear right and return to the car park and starting point.

Other information

Whitesands Bay has a shop and café, public toilets, emergency and BT telephones, as well as a seasonal lifeguard hut and First Aid point. There is also a camping and caravan site, and a youth hostel nearby.

Ramsey island sunset

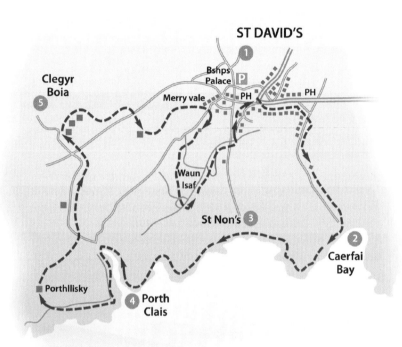

Walk 10
St David's and Porth Clais

Walk details

Approx distance:	*6 miles/9.5 kilometres*
Approx time:	*3 hours*
O.S. Maps:	*1:25 000 North Pembrokeshire Outdoor Leisure 35*
Start:	*Cross Square in the centre of St David's.*
Access:	*St David's is at the end of the A487 Haverfordwest and Fishguard roads. Buses 342, 400 (the Puffin Shuttle), 404 (the Strumble Shuttle), 411 and 413 all stop at St David's. Local city bus 403 the Celtic Coaster calls at Porth Clais in season.*
Parking:	*There is free parking in the Pebbles (the road leading down to the cathedral from Cross Square). Other signposted car parks in and around St David's. Parking also possible at Caerfai Bay and Porth Clais.*
Going:	*Moderate – coastal path, farm track, green lane.*

1. St David's

St David founded his church and monastery in the mid 6th century, though nothing remains of the foundations. Property was held in common, with emphasis on prayer and simple sustenance through water and a primarily vegetarian diet. David himself is believed to have travelled widely before establishing his community, helping to establish centres at Glastonbury, Bath and Gloucester, and, according to legend, travelling to Jerusalem in the company of other local saints where he was given an altar stone by the Patriarch. He died March 1st possibly in 589 or 601. The

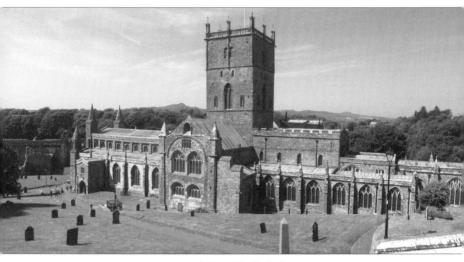

St David's Cathedra

settlement survived the frequent Viking raids, but it's importance was seen as a threat by the incoming Normans, who imposed their own pattern of cathedral and diocese. William the Conqueror paid homage here in 1081. According to tradition David himself was canonized by Pope Calixtus II in 1123. The present cathedral, Wales' finest church, was begun in 1181, reaching it's final building phase by the early 16th century when the tower was raised to it's present height by Bishop Vaughan. There is a fine and unique oak ceiling in the nave, it's initial phase of construction dating from the 1530s. It is of Renaissance styling, and has been attributed to Flemish craftsmen. Recent examination of the roof has suggested that it is of Welsh oak. Poor foundations

Cathedral misericord

the west wall of the nave and it's arcade pillars to lean outwards; thus a wooden ceiling rather than a stone vault. Of the delightful carvings under the Choir misericords (ledged seats allowing infirm priests support during offices which required them to stand) twenty-one can be dated to approximately the late 15th century; the seven others are Victorian replacements. They offer a fine commentary on medieval life, humour and imagination. The original cathedral city would have been surrounded by a 14th century wall interspersed with four gatehouses; the Tower Gatehouse is the only one to survive. Pilgrims, arriving by road and sea, flocked to St David's throughout the Middle Ages. On the pilgrimage route from Ireland to Santiago de Compostela in Spain via Wales, Cornwall and Brittany, it was said that two pilgrimages to St David's was equal to one to Rome, three the equal of one to Jerusalem. Following the Reformation the cathedral nearly fell into ruin, requiring restoration in 1763, and again between 1862 and 1877 when Gilbert Scott redesigned the west front more in accord with it's medieval appearance. New cloisters were built between 2004 and 2007. St David's is unique in that the reigning sovereign is a canon of the cathedral and chapter. The ruined Bishop's Palace nearby was largely built between 1280 and 1350 by Bishop Gower. Abetted by the Reformation the Palace was derelict by the 18th century. Recognising St David's continuing importance it was awarded city status in 1995; it is the United Kingdom's smallest city.

2. Caerfai Bay

Caerfai has a fine stretch of sand at low tides, making it St David's local beach. Popular with locals and visitors it's cliffs also afford space for coasteers, the sport that combines swimming with cliff exploration – jumping off the

Caerfai Bay

rocks into the sea is part of the fun. Along with neighbouring Caer Bwdy it's quarries provided it's distinctive purplish stone for the cathedral; nearby Caer Bwdy's quarry was re-opened as recently as 1996 when sufficient stone was quarried for repair work for the cathedral's west front and any future building work.

3. St Non's

St David was born here, reputedly in a thunderstorm, on the site now occupied by St Non's chapel, in around 520. It is said that Non's Well (sited inland, just off the Coast Path) sprang forth at his birth. St Non, the saint's mother, went to Brittany shortly after the birth. Her tomb is in the chapel of

St Non's chapel

Dirinon in Finistère. His father was reputed to be Sant, a Ceredigion chief. St Non's Retreat was built in 1929, the Chapel of Our Lady and St Non in 1934.

4. Porth Clais

Porth Clais has always been the harbour for St David's, and was at one time under the ownership of the church – *porth* is the Welsh word for port, *clais*, it has been argued, stands for a monastic community. St David was baptized here at the head of the creek by Elvis, Bishop of Munster; there is a well on the site, where at one time it is believed a chapel also stood. Cathedral records show coal and limestone being landed here as early as 1384. Caerfai and Caer Bwdi's purple stone was landed here for the cathedral, as was the oak for the roof of the nave. Later imports included general merchandise and timber from Ireland, with exports of corn, malt and wool. Bristol became a much favoured port of call with local corn going to help feed the city's growing population. Ships, most with purpose built flat bottoms, would have been beached here and their cargoes unloaded onto waiting carts. There is in the cathedral a misericord carving of a typical 14th and 15th century cargo ship of the type that would have visited Porth Clais being repaired by shipwrights. The breakwater, possibly Norman in origin, was extensively repaired in the 18th century.

The lime kilns on the old trading quays would have been in constant use. The limestone burnt in the kilns was taken by horse and cart for spreading on the fields, and for use as mortar. Lime as mortar was used in the construction of the cathedral, though the lime for this would probably have been burnt in kilns at the cathedral site. The restored kilns here were in constant use from 1650 to 1900. As well as providing a safe haven for trade and shelter Porth Clais' natural harbour was favoured by the occasional marauding

Norseman, intent on sacking St David's semi-monastic settlement. The Mabinogion, that gem of medieval Welsh tales, notes Porth Clais as the landing place of the mythical boar, Twrch Trwyth, hotly pursued by Arthur. Later more materialistic ages would have seen the odd smuggler or two, often combining his activities with legitimate trade. The last imports to the harbour were of coal, required up to the 1950s to supply the city's gasworks, now demolished, and which stood on the site of the present car park. The inlet is still a busy place, popular now with the outdoor enthusiast, whether water borne or rock climber.

Porth Clais

5. Clegyr Boia (*Boia's Rock*)

Boia was an Irish chieftain and contemporary of St David who built his stronghold on the rock outcrop overlooking the peninsula. He came into conflict with St David when David decided to move his religious house from the shadow of Carn Llidi, the rock outcrop at St David's Head, to the banks of the river Alun. Legend has it that Boia's wife taunted St David and the local monks by having her maids disport themselves in the river *with bodies bare*. Undeterred St David finally persuaded Boia to grant him the land on which the cathedral now stands. Boia himself was killed and his stronghold destroyed by a fellow Irish chieftain Lisci or Lysgi, who gives his name to Porthlysgi Bay around the coast from Porth Clais.

Excavations undertaken here in 1902 and 1942 showed that the site had been in occupation during the Neolithic period. Traces of timber huts, pottery, stone axes and flint scrapers were found – it is one of the very few Neolithic settlements to have been found in Wales. The settlers here may well have made use of the two burial chambers to be found at Carn Llidi and St David's Head. Archaeologists have determined how a Neolithic house built on the hill would have looked – set between two rock walls it's wooden roof would have been supported by eight timber posts. Excavation also showed that the site was in use at a later date, possibly Iron Age, or possibly it is Boia's settlement. Built in the early Iron Age tradition, stone faced ramparts would have enclosed the hill top. The gate, sited on the south-western slope, was found on excavation to have guard recesses on it's inner side. Well worth taking the short track to the summit for the superb views of the landscape, with the cathedral tucked away safely in the valley of Merry Vale.

Walk directions: [-] indicates history note

1. Starting from Cross Sqaure in the centre of St David's [1], and passing the city's 14th century cross (restored in the 1870s) continue up High Street. Bear right into Feidr Pant-y-Bryn (*hollow of the hill lane*) – the Tourist Information Centre to your left is worth a visit, both for it's architectural design and it's art gallery, shop and café.

2. At the end of the lane turn right into the Caerfai road and continue on to Caerfai Bay [2]. From the car park head down steps to join the Coast Path and continue right, via St Non's [3], to reach Porth Clais [4].

3. At Porth Clais continue on the Coast Path, past the restored lime kilns, to reach a kissing gate on the headland. Choice of two paths – take the right hand path and continue ahead with the fence to your immediate right. The Coast Path heads off to the left.

4. Where the path bears left turn right to reach a farm gate. Go ahead on a permissive path to reach Porthllisky farm – as a permissive path the farmer does have the right to close access, but this is unlikely! Bear right onto a farm track and continue to reach the minor road leading uphill from Porth Clais.

St Non's well

5. Bear left and continue to reach a crossroads. Go ahead to bear right at Clegyr Boia [5] onto a signposted bridleway and follow the track as it continues past buildings to reach a minor road. Bear left and continue on the road a short distance, bearing right onto a signposted bridleway – also sign for Felin Isaf.

6. Continue to Felin Isaf. Just past here, after a gate, there is a footpath ascending up steps – ignore and continue

Bear right at Clegyr Boia and follow the track

ahead on the bridleway through Merry Vale to reach a minor road by Glanalan. Bear right. Continue past the houses to bear left onto the wet heath of Waun Isaf (Lower Moor) – cattle grid here, and signpost for St David's City walk.

7. Continue across the moor and a field to meet a path. Bear left and continue uphill to reach the access road to St Non's and Warpool Court hotel. Continue ahead and almost immediately bear left onto a path. Continue to reach residential houses. Continue ahead on Bryn Road, to bear left along Mitre Lane to reach Goat Street – Cross Square and starting point is to your right.

Other information

All available in and around St David's. The cathedral has shops, café, and a gallery and treasury, where the cathedral's treasures are exhibited. The National Park's Tourist Information Centre also houses a café and an art gallery, with permanent exhibitions of the work of Graham Sutherland who worked in the county – the centre is well worth a visit just to view it's original architecture. Twr y Felin offers outdoor pursuits, and the Thousand Islands Expeditions shop exploration of the coast and the offshore islands by boat. St David's City Walk is a short leafleted National Trust walk taking in both the city and the variety of habitats to be found around the city – shop and visitor centre close to the City Cross.

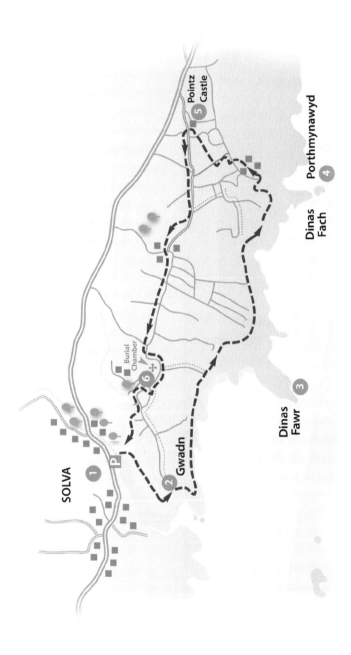

Walk 11
Solva

Walk details

Approx distance: *5.5 miles/8.75 kilometres*

Approx time: *3 hours*

O.S. Maps: *1:25 000 North Pembrokeshire Outdoor Leisure 35*

Start: *Car park in Lower Solva, in front of the Harbour Inn.*

Access: *Solva is 2½ miles/4 kilometres south-east of St David's on the A487 St David's to Newgale and Haverfordwest main road. Buses 400 the Puffin Shuttle and 411 stop at Solva.*

Parking: *Car park in Lower Solva – seasonal charge. Limited parking also possible at Pointz Castle.*

Going: *Moderate – mostly coastal path, field, farm track and minor road.*

1. Solva (Solfach)

Solva's harbour owes it's origins to it's history as a meltwater channel of the ice sheet that once covered the area; when sea levels rose it created a ria, a drowned valley. It's delightful setting makes it one of the most popular villages in the county. It's sheltered harbour, despite a dangerous entrance, has made it St Brides Bay's safest port of call. There has been much speculation over the origins of the name. Those who favour Norse origins point out that in Norse *sölv ö* can mean silver island, or *sol vo* a sunny harbour or fjord, as well as *sölva*, samphire. However the earliest references are to Salfach, closer to Solva's Welsh name of Solfach.

Solva, the Gribin, and Gwadn

Solva's recorded importance as a trading and commercial centre really begins in the 17th century with exports of wheat and malt, and imports of timber, cloth and oar blades. With the establishment of a shipping company in 1756 Solva entered it's period of prosperity. Unlike near neighbour Porth Clais, which could only handle vessels up to 100 tons, Solva could cater for ships of 500 tons, and by 1800 there were some thirty vessels of 20 to 250 tons here, as well as the beginnings of a shipbuilding industry. There were nine warehouses built to house corn and butter for export to particularly Bristol, though also to Ireland, and coal and limestone were brought in to fertilize the corn basket of St David's peninsula. The restored lime kilns at the head of the beach (the rectangular section being the former lime burner's hut) contributed their share of lime for the fields. Richard Fenton, Pembrokeshire's historian, describes the effect of two of Solva's former eleven kilns *whose hot vapour and dust and noise incident to them, make them very offensive, proving a great drawback on a residence on*

Solva

that part of the town where the chief shops and warehouses are ... Trade had peaked by the mid 19th century, and with the coming of the railways quieter (until tourism!) and less polluted times were ahead for Solva. The last regular boat service to Bristol was finally discontinued in 1914.

Solva was host to the construction of two lighthouses for the Smalls, two notorious rocks projecting out into the Irish Sea to the west of Grassholm island's gannet colony. The first, a curious shed like affair resting on iron and oak stanchions, was constructed in the 1770s to a design by a Liverpool violin maker, Henry Whitesides. He had been the winner of a competition launched by a group of Liverpool merchants who had become frustrated at the loss of Liverpool ships on the Smalls and the reefs of the nearby Hats and Barrels. A new lighthouse of Bodmin granite was chipped and dressed on the purpose built Trinity Quay, and taken out by tug for assembly on site in 1861. Trinity Quay was home to the Solva lifeboat, the *Charles and Mary Egerton*, from 1869 until 1887, when she was sold; the St David's lifeboat being preferred.

2. Gwadn

Despite the pebble ridge there is a fine expanse of golden sand at low tide. From here the nature of the difficulties facing anyone entering Solva's sheltered harbour become apparent, for guarding the entrance are St Elvis and Black Rocks. There was, until comparatively recently, a pilot to assist visiting vessels, and leading marks were painted on the two rocks, with two further marks inland. In 1882 Black Rock, the major obstacle, was painted white with lime to assist returning mariners. Despite the dangers wrecks have been rare; perhaps the worst disaster concerned the *Phoebe and Mary*, en route from Philadelphia to Liverpool in 1773. Despite rescue by a Solva boat the returning vessel struck Black Rock with the loss of sixty lives, including seven Solva men. One transatlantic vessel with a happier fate was the *Cradle*, which sailed from Solva in 1848 direct to New York for the princely sum of £3! The Gribin – possibly named from *crib*, the Welsh for ridge – divides the two valleys of

Gwadn and the Gribin

Solva and the Gribin stream, that of Solva being the deeper, and, like the Milford Haven, a classic example of a drowned valley. There was an Iron Age fort on Gribin Point, with a settlement further inland, overlooking Lower Solva.

3. Dinas Fawr

Rather difficult to believe now but the headland here at Dinas Fawr was mined for lead and silver for some two and a half centuries. No doubt there was some surface mining during the Bronze Age, but the first real attempt to mine below the surface dates from the 1620s. Operating as St Elvis lead mine there were further attempts until final failure in 1869. Ore extracted during the late 18th century was taken down to Gwadn where the then owner, Thomas Williams, had his storehouse. Most of the tunnels and adits are now sealed, but there are visible spoil heaps and levels adjacent to the Coast Path. There are sandy beaches close by, at Aber-west and Porth y Bwch, but access is problematic – though I have seen a fox ambling down the cliff without too much trouble!

4. Dinas Fach

Dinas Fach is an impressive narrow promontory jutting out into St Brides Bay. It is fronted by a turf covered island with

Sunset over Dinas Fawr and Dinas Fach

the attractive sand beach of Porthmynawyd to one side. Rarely crowded in summer! The short springy turf of the headland is ideal feeding territory for those rarities of the crow family, the choughs, with their distinctive black coats and red beak and legs. The coastal section above Stacen y Brenin (*the King's Stack*), between Dinas Fawr and Dinas Fach, is ideal for the linnets, who congregate here in their red and chestnut finery during the summer months.

5. Pointz Castle

Pointz Castle, of which only the motte, or mound, survives, is believed to take it's name from Poncius, a 12th century Norman knight and tenant of the then Bishop of St David's, Peter de Leia. Much of the land here would once have been the property of the Bishop. Early Norman castles would have been simple affairs. The motte, a flattened mound of earth surrounded by a ditch, would have a wooden watchtower protected by a circular palisade of pointed stakes. Connected to it was the bailey, or court, similarly protected by ditch and fence, where the living quarters and stables would be housed. These wooden castles gradually gave way to the great stone castles which heralded Norman overlordship.

6. St Elvis burial chamber

The two St Elvis cromlechau, or burial chambers, date back some 5,000 years. Used by Neolithic peoples for collective burials they would have originally been covered by earth or stones to form a barrow. Long after their purpose had been forgotten they became the subject of legend and prophecy. Graves of giants and heroes, it was said that if you were to walk around one on the night of the full moon you would see the face of your lover. To sleep in one meant madness, or the silver tongued gift of poetry. The word cromlech seems to have been first used by Pembrokeshire's Elizabethan historian, George Owen, *crwm llech* meaning curved stone. Often the Breton term, dolmen (stone table), is used to describe them. There was at one time a chapel dedicated to St Teilo close by, though by the late 18th century it had fallen into disuse. However the font has been rescued, saved from it's new use as a pig trough!

Walk directions: [-] indicates history note
1.   Starting from the car park in front of the Harbour Inn in Lower Solva [1] cross the footbridge over the stream.
2.   Join the Coast Path, either as it ascends the Gribin above the barred tunnel (constructed in the 1950s to carry materials for the construction of a Treatment works in the neighbouring valley), or above the lime kilns at the head of the beach. Continue along the Gribin to the beach at Gwadn [2]. Alternatively, if the tide is well out, it is possible to walk on the sand around to Gwadn from the starting point, though you may have to wade!
3.   From Gwadn continue on the Coast Path across fields to Dinas Fawr [3]. Great views open up across St Brides Bay. Continue on to Dinas Fach and the sheltered sandy beach of Porthmynawyd [4].
4.   From Porthmynawyd leave the coast and head inland on a clearly defined path. Just past a ruined cottage on the right turn left and cross a stream by a footbridge and ascend to a field. Go though the gate into the field and keeping to the right field edge continue to reach gates on the right. Continue across the field keeping to the left edge to a kissing gate.
5.   Cross the farm track to a gate and follow the path around

to the left to reach another gate and the road at Pointz Castle [5]. Turn left and continue to Lochvane. At Lochvane continue ahead to reach a green lane – the bridleway right leads to the main A487.

Starting from the car park in front of the Harbour Inn in Lower Solva

6. Continue ahead on green lane and field to reach the farm lane to St Elvis farm. The route continues on the farm track adjacent to the lane. Just before the farm buildings turn left and continue on the path fenced off from a farm track. Just before the fenced path ends turn right through a wooden gate – the fenced-off area in front protects St Elvis' burial chamber [6].

7. Continue ahead on a farm track, keeping the burial chambers to your left, to meet a kissing gate. Continuing on the farm track shortly reach a kissing gate on the right. Choice here of continuing on the farm track to Gwadn, and back to Solva along the Gribin, or of bearing right and continuing across the field.

8. If turning right keep to the right field edge to another kissing gate. Turn immediately left, go through the gate ahead, and continue along the wooded valley slope. After a short distance the path emerges into more open scrubland. Bear right and continue downhill to reach a stream.

9. Cross the stream by a wooden footbridge and bear diagonally left. Continue uphill on a zig-zag path to reach the top of the Gribin at two wooden gates to your left.

10. Either continue ahead on the Gribin, to shortly bear right and downhill to Solva and the starting point, or bear right before the second gate, keep to the left field edge and shortly bear left downhill on a steepish path, also to Lower Solva.

Other information

Most available in Solva. Middle Mill, just north of Solva, has both a woollen and a corn mill.

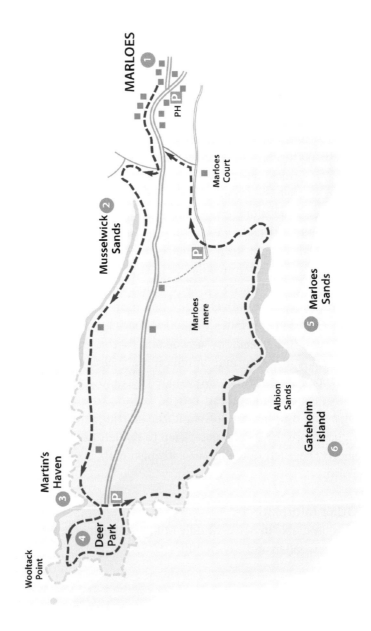

Walk 12
Marloes

Walk details
Approx distance: *7 miles/11 kilometres*

Approx time: *3 hours*

O.S. Maps: *OS 1:25 000 South Pembrokeshire Outdoor Leisure 36*

Start: *Marloes*

Access: *Marloes is one mile/0.75 kilometres west of the B4327 Haverfordwest to Dale road. Buses 315/400 Haverfordwest to Marloes and Dale (Puffin Shuttle).*

Parking: *Parking possible in Marloes, or else there is a small parking bay just by the footpath turning to Musselwick. National Trust car parks also at Marloes Sands and Martin's Haven.*

Going: *Moderate – mostly coastal path.*

1. Marloes
Marloes has the distinction of being the most westerly village in Wales – from here the road leads only to the Deer Park. It derives it's name from the welsh, moel rhos, ie *bare moor*. Yet despite it's Welsh linguistic heritage it shows similarity in layout with English villages, and with other similar villages in south Pembrokeshire. The local church, St Peters, was restored in the 1870s. One noticeable architectural feature is the clock tower, built in 1904 by Lady Kensington, widow of William, the 4th Lord Kensington, who died in 1896. A plaque on the tower notes it's erection by members of the Pembrokeshire Liberal Association. It is said to have been built as a reminder of Lord Kensington's punctuality. As Barons of Kensington the Edwardes family noted their Pembrokeshire interests on

Marloes

Marloes clock tower

the London map; Marloes Road vies with Edwardes Square, Pembroke Road with Nevern Place. Marloes mere, drained and now a wetland, at one time provided London's Harley Street medical practitioners with medicinal leeches.

2. Musselwick

Musselwick Sands, tucked away out of reach of the prevailing south westerlies, has a fine sandy beach. Good swimming, and fewer crowds than at the better known Marloes Sands. Beware of being cut off by an incoming tide, these are not the cliffs to climb in a hurry! At the beginning of the Mesolithic era Musselwick would have been well inland, but with the demise of the great northern ice fields the peats, woods and marshes favoured by Mesolithic hunters vanished slowly under the sea – the soft red sandstones fell victim to the waves, while the hard volcanic rocks of the Deer Park and St David's Head stood resistant, and remain to frame St Brides Bay.

From Musselwick north to nearby Nab Head the soft reds and purples mingle with the harder black shales; at Musselwick itself the uniform black of the rocky path down to the beach confirms the change to harder rock. Excavations at Nab Head have revealed the site of a

Musselwick

Mesolithic/Neolithic flint chipping factory. Axe and arrow heads, simple tools including scraping tools for cleaning skins, as well as unusually for a site of this type, more than six hundred perforated beads, have been found. There are displays in Tenby museum.

3. Martin's Haven

From Martin's Haven, Marloes' harbour, boats leave for the islands of Skomer and Skokholm, home to one of the great bird shows of Britain. Don't miss it! At one time Marloes fishermen sailed out to camp on Grassholm's gannet island in search of lobster and crayfish. Sea birds provided good bait; and eating. Nowadays the gannets are left strictly to themselves. During the construction of the public toilets in the 1980s a stone cross, dated to between AD 600 to 900 was unearthed, and is now housed in the wall flanking the path down to the beach.

4. The Deer Park

Despite it's name the Deer Park has never held deer; a walled enclosure, still extant, was built alongside the valley running from Martin's Haven across the park in the 18th century to house them, but it was never put to purpose. The high bank and ditch above the valley inside the park formed

Martin's Haven

a defensive feature of a former Iron Age settlement. The bracken and gorse are kept to manageable lengths by Welsh mountain ponies – areas of close cropped grassland are much favoured by the local choughs, a common siting with their distinctive red legs and beaks a fine contrast to their black crow's sheen. The beaches around the Deer Park provide good pupping grounds for the local seals during autumn. Well worth walking up to Wooltack Point for the excellent views over Skomer island and St Brides Bay. Jack Sound, between the point and Midland Isle has a fearsome reputation, it's tide races leading to disaster for many ships – nearby Albion Sands takes it's name from the wreck of the packet *Albion*, run ashore after she was holed on a rock in the sound in 1837; two iron shafts of her remain, pointing to heaven.

Deer Park seals

St Brides Bay from the Deer Park

5. Marloes Sands

One of the finest and most picturesque beaches in Wales the sands are a fine place to spent an afternoon's sunbathing during the summer months, and provide good swimming. One notable geological feature of the sands is the Three Chimneys – beds of Silurian sandstone and mudstone upended to stand vertically, the three 'slabs' easily identifiable. The feature film Snow White and the Huntsman was filmed here, the sands echoing to horses' hooves.

Marloes Sands

6. Gateholm island and Watery Bay fort

The Old Red Sandstone rock of Gateholm island (from the Norse *goat island*) is home to a ruined settlement, perhaps established when the island could have been a promontory of the Marloes peninsula. Finds of Roman pottery and coins from the 3rd or 4th century date had suggested that at least some of the settlement could be dated to the later Roman

Gateholm island

period. Gateholm itself and a promontory fort on the coast at nearby Watery Bay were excavated by Channel 4's Time Team in 2011 to investigate the site's pedigree. Given Gateholm's inaccessibility a zip wire between the island and coast was required to transport people and equipment. Excavation showed that the site had been in use in prehistory, later to be remodelled and reused in the late Roman and early Christian periods. Watery Bay fort excavations showed it to have been a substantial construction, it still has clearly visible defensive banks, and it was in use at the same time as Gateholm; however by the Roman period it had fallen out of use.

Walk directions: [-] indicates history note
1. Starting from Marloes [**1**] walk up the minor road leading to the Deer Park. After a short distance, by a rough parking bay, bear right across a stile and continue to reach both the Coast Path and the path leading down to Musselwick Sands [**2**].
2. Bear left to join the Coast Path and continue on to Martin's Haven [**3**], embarkation point for the islands. The Coast Path continues around the Deer Park [**4**], though there is a short cut across the neck of the park if preferred.
3. Continue on to Marloes Sands [**5**], passing Watery Bay fort and Gateholm island [**6**] en route – there is a rough

track leading down to the sands on the Marloes side of the peninsula overlooking Gateholm.

4. Once at Marloes Sands leave the Coast Path and take the path leading up from the beach to reach a minor road. Bear right and continue the short distance to reach Marloes Court on the right. Bear left on a footpath and cross fields to reach the minor road leading back to Marloes. Bear right to regain the starting point.

Continue on to Martin's Haven

Other information

Post office and shop and pub in Marloes. Public toilets and telephone opposite the Lobster Pot Inn, and public toilets also at Martin's Haven. There is a hide overlooking Marloes mere – easily

Skomer island puffins

reached on the path leading past the youth hostel at Marloes Sands. Lockley Lodge at Martin's Haven has a gift shop, and sells tickets for the crossing to Skomer island.

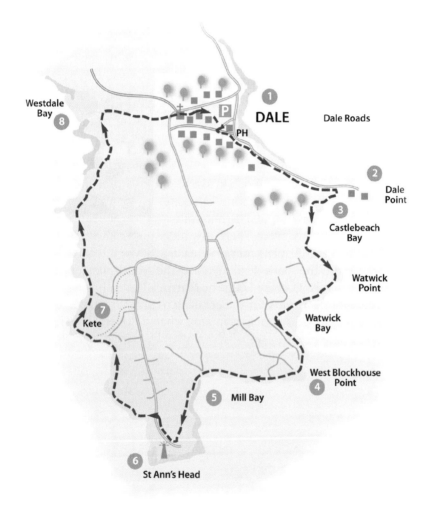

Westdale
Bay
8

DALE
1
P
PH
Dale Roads

Dale
Point
2

Castlebeach
Bay
3

Watwick
Point

Watwick
Bay

Kete
7

West Blockhouse
Point
4

Mill Bay
5

St Ann's Head
6

Walk 13
Dale

Walk details

Approx distance: *7 miles/11 kilometres*

Approx time: *3¼ hours*

O.S. Maps: *OS 1:25 000 South Pembrokeshire Outdoor Leisure 36*

Start: *Dale*

Access: *Dale is 11 miles from Haverfordwest on the B4327, and is within easy reach of Broad Haven and Little Haven, and St Brides Haven and Marloes. Buses 315/400 operate from Haverfordwest to Dale (Puffin Shuttle).*

Parking: *Dale car park – on the right as you enter Dale; seasonal charge.*

Going: *Moderate – a little road walking, but mostly coastal path.*

1. Dale

Dale's written history begins in 1293 when a Robert de Vale was granted a charter to hold a weekly market and an annual fair. The present castle, a private residence, probably occupies the original castle's site. The medieval church, with it's 15th century tower, is dedicated to St James, and was substantially restored in the 1890s. By Tudor times Dale was a place of some importance, certainly so far as the Milford Haven is concerned Dale and Angle, on the opposite shore, were the largest villages, with Dale vying with Fishguard for size. Three eight to nine ton trading ships were owned, and Dale became known in Liverpool and Bristol for it's fine ale. Fortunes seem to have declined by the 1800s however, with the village fallen into ruins, but by the 1850s two ships totalling forty three tons had been built, and fishing, shipbuilding and general trading were again to

Dale

Dale Point

Castlebeach Bay

the fore. The four prominent buildings overlooking the bay and which line what was once Dale's quay all date from the 17th/18th centuries. Whilst Dale is noted as the sunniest place in Wales, the Dale peninsula makes up for it by being one of the windiest in Britain! Dale's forté is now water sports, though there is still good ale to be had. Often used as an overnight anchorage by ocean going yachts, Dale Roads played host to many of the finest sailing ships in the world during the Tall Ships race in 1991.

2. Dale Point

There was an Iron Age fort here by 300 BC – the single bank and ditch are clearly visible, running out across the headland, with the former entrance in the middle of the bank. Dale Fort was built as part of Milford Haven's 19th century defensive system between 1852 and 1856, the road leading to it from Dale being the old military access road. The fort was taken over in 1947 by the Field Studies Council who run courses mainly in marine biology, though geology, geography, archaeology and painting also find a place. Good views from the headland over Dale Roads.

3. Castlebeach Bay

Castlebeach is a pleasant wooded bay with a sandy beach. There is an old lime kiln at the head of the beach where limestone quarried at West Williamston, near Lawrenny, or on Caldey island, would have been burnt to provide lime for local farms as fertilizer or mortar. Now overgrown there are the ruins of the lime burner's cottage in the wood. Lime burning had largely died out by the beginning of the 20th century, the last recorded use of kilns in the Dale area was at Pickleridge in the 1920s.

4. West Blockhouse Point

West Blockhouse Point derives it's name from the Victorian fort built here as part of Milford Haven's fortifications. The first attempt to fortify the Haven was undertaken by Henry VIII, with blockhouses on both northern and southern sides of the Haven entrance, but of these only that at Angle survives. Further fortifications had to wait until the mid 19th century when fears of French invasion led to a more thorough system. West Blockhouse was matched by another fort, now demolished, on the opposite shore, by Rat island at East Angle; Dale Fort was matched by the island fort on Thorn island; the circular island fort on Stack Rock by Popton Fort, by Angle Bay; and so on down the Haven, until the Defensible Barracks, holding the main defence force of five hundred men, was reached at the new Royal Naval Dockyard at Pembroke Dock. The whole system, complete by 1875, was overseen by General Gordon of Khartoum fame. Obsolete as soon as built, and without a shot having been fired, these forts became known as Palmerston's Follies – after Palmerston, at various times Prime Minister and Foreign Secretary during mid century. The fort here was built by 1857 for eighty men, and was at last utilized during both World Wars, for anti-aircraft defence. By 1950 the fort was abandoned, and is now the property of the Landmark Trust, in use for holiday letting.

The three navigation towers, together with that on

Watwick Point, were built in 1970. By holding the central tower here in transit with that on Watwick Point, shipping is led into the deep water channel. There is a similar system of buildings and towers on Great Castle Head for the next deep channel section. The Master of the vessel aligns the lights, or the white or black lines. At night the lights have a possible range of nineteen miles/thirty kilometres, the red lights on the two outer towers here indicating the channel entrance. Watwick Point tower currently ranks as one of the tallest lighthouses in the world. They are under the jurisdiction of the Milford Haven Port Authority.

5. Mill Bay

Mill Bay, just before sunset on Sunday 7 August 1485, was the unlikely host to the beginnings of one of the great adventures of British history, when Henry Tudor came ashore from Brittany, with his fleet of fifty thousand ships and four thousand men landing at nearby Dale, to begin his lightning march to Stafford, Bosworth Field, and the English crown. Born in nearby Pembroke Castle in 1459, Henry had been left sole heir to the Lancastrian throne following the Wars of the Roses, and had had to seek refuge in France. Recalled in 1485 Henry landed on home territory to meet enthusiastic support, many hailing him as the new King Arthur. By 22 August Richard III was dead, the Tudor age inaugurated, and Henry VII on the throne.

The wreck here is that of a boom defence vessel which broke away from the tug towing it for scrap in 1964. One earlier disaster from the days of sail – the Mill Bay disaster – occurred in September 1866. The leader of a group of six or seven sailing

Mill Bay

ships running before a gale in poor visibility went aground – the others followed suit with disastrous loss of life.

West Blockhouse

6. St Ann's Head

There was once a small chapel here, dedicated to St Ann, mother of Mary and patron saint of Brittany, and quite possibly established by Henry VII in thanks for his victory at Bosworth Field. There was a twenty foot/six metres high tower light attached to the chapel, a great boon to ships entering the Haven. However the chapel was demolished during the Reformation, though the tower light was rebuilt. A second lighthouse was built in 1714, which comprised two towers lit by coal. The front tower was rebuilt further inland in 1841, and was modernised in 1958 when it was put onto electricity. The rear light became the coastguard station in 1910. The small tower house contains the foghorn. The old coastguard and Trinity House cottages and the coastguard station are now in private ownership. The walled garden and stone quay nearby date from 1800, the latter built for transporting materials for the lighthouse. A new thin steel towered lighthouse was built out at sea, just off the Head, in 1966, to mark the entrance to the deep water channel – the Mid Channel Rocks Lighthouse.

The area between St Ann's Head, across to the Angle peninsula and flat topped Linney Head, is known locally as the Heads. Some 100,000 years ago the Bristol Channel was mostly land, and the river then flowing through the Haven would have continued across the plain to join the Severn almost halfway between St Ann's Head and Lands End in Cornwall, but with the end of the Ice Age the meltwater

St Ann's Head

Skomer island at sunset

flooded the Haven, creating a ria, or drowned river valley, much along present lines. The mouth of the Haven is one and a quarter miles/two kilometres wide, and eighteen miles/thirty kilometres long, navigable as far as Haverfordwest and Canaston Bridge. The decision to create a major oil port was taken in the late 1950s, Esso the first refinery to open in 1960. Some veritable giants of tankers are now common fare; however there are some that come to grief. In October 1978 the Greek tanker *Christos Bitas* went aground on the Hats and Barrels reef, near Grassholm island, spilling thirty five thousand tons of oil. As a result of this incident the Centre for Oiled Birds was established at West Williamston, near Carew. The Centre was well occupied in February 1996 when the *Sea Empress* went aground on the shoals and rocks below St Ann's Head, spilling seventy thousand tons of light crude oil in the six days it took to tow her off the rocks.

7. Bird islands and HMS Harrier

Great views from here of the islands of Skokholm, Grassholm and Skomer – life on this side of the peninsula is much quieter than the activity and bustle of the Haven. Ronald Lockley made Skokholm his island home from 1927 to 1939, establishing Britain's first bird observatory there in 1933. His two books, *Dream Island* and *Island Days*, describe his life, where he *resolved to imitate [Thoreau's] austere mode of living when I at last came to dwell on my dream island.* Together with Skomer and Grassholm these islands represent some of the finest seabird colonies in Europe, with shearwaters, gannets, razorbills, guillemots, choughs and the splendid puffins. They can be reached from Martin's Haven, near Marloes. During the medieval period the islands provided it's owners with a good steady income derived from the farming of rabbits. In the ownership of Dale Castle estate since 1646 Skokholm was bought, following the death of the last owner in 2005, by the Wildlife Trust of South and West Wales in 2006. Acquisition of the lighthouse and surrounding land in 2012 has completed the Trust's ownership of the whole island.

Kete was the site of HMS Harrier, a Royal Navy radar and meteorological school, which closed in 1960. The land was bought by the National Trust in 1967, buildings cleared, and the area returned to agricultural use. The former married quarters in Dale are now private residences. In it's heyday Kete was used to train radar technicians and fighter direction officers, whose task it was to detect enemy aircraft prior to their attack on friendly shipping, and to direct fighter planes to deal with them. Mock battles were fought over the local seaways out to the Smalls lighthouse. In it's early days there were no aircraft that could be spared for training purposes so former Walls ice cream tricycles became a useful weapon of war – one set of trikes became an enemy bomber, it's course steered by compass, whilst the others, once the enemy trikes had been spotted by the radar operator, were sent to attack them. They were later replaced by the real planes and electronic simulators. The base provided for some eight hundred people. There is a memorial plaque, with a photograph of the site, in Kete car park.

St Brides Bay with Grassholm island in the far distance

Westdale Bay and Skokholm island

Watwick Bay

8. Westdale Bay

Unlike Dale Westdale Bay has a sandy beach, but beware of the strong undertow on the ebb tide if you are planning to swim. Overlooking the bay on the south side is the Iron Age fort on Great Castle Head, dating from circa 100 BC. It has massive banks and ditches, and is particularly impressive on the approach from Kete. The entrance makes good use of the rock faulting. To the north, again overlooking the bay, are the remains of the old Dale airfield, which was to transfer to Brawdy, near Newgale. The route from Westdale back to Dale follows the course of an old river valley, and, but for the fall in sea level, Dale peninsula would have remained an island.

Walk directions: [-] indicates history note
1. Starting from Dale [1] walk past the Griffin Inn and Dale Yacht Club and follow the tarmac road to Dale Fort Field Centre.
2. Just before the Field Centre views open up, left, over Dale Roads. To the right access to the coastal path and the headland overlooking Dale Point [2].
3. Follow the Coast Path from Dale Point on to Castlebeach Bay [3], and continue on past the navigation beacon on Watwick Point to the sandy beach of Watwick Bay – a popular bay in summer. Access to the beach down a narrow footpath.

4. Continue to West Blockhouse Point [**4**], and Mill Bay's small rocky inlet [**5**], to arrive at St Ann's Head, [**6**] guarding the entrance to the Milford Haven.

5. The tarmac road leads two miles/three kilometres back to Dale – continue however the two and a half miles/four kilometres on the Coast Path around to Kete [**7**] and Westdale Bay [**8**].

6. From Westdale Bay – easy access to the beach down convenient steps – cross the stone stile to the right of the Coast Path, and continue inland across the centre of the field to join the farm track leading to Hayguard Hay farm.

Follow the Coast Path to Castlebeach Bay

7. Continue ahead on the farm track to shortly join the road leading back into Dale and the starting point. Choice of road, or footpath across the fields by Dale car park.

Other information

Free parking in the National Trust car park at Kete – there is no official car parking at St Ann's Head. Limited parking is also possible in the parking bay above Westdale Bay – follow the road behind Dale Castle. All facilities are available in Dale. A very popular centre for water sports.

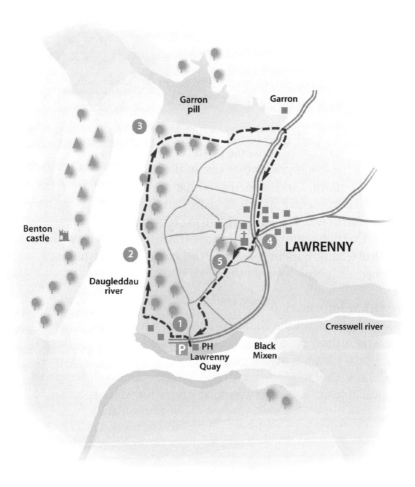

Walk 14
Lawrenny

Walk details

Approx distance: *3 miles/4.75 kilometres*

Approx time: *1¼ hours*

O.S. Maps: *OS 1:25 000 South Pembrokeshire Outdoor Leisure 36*

Start: *Lawrenny Quay*

Access: *Lawrenny can be reached from the A4075 Carew to Canaston Bridge road, either following the minor road from Cresselly, or from Cross Hands near Oakwood. Just follow the Lawrenny signposts. Nearest bus service 361 stops at Cresswell Quay 2½ miles/4 kilometres distant. May be a limited seasonal service to Lawrenny – check with Tourist Information Centres for any details.*

Parking: *Parking bay by the Yacht station. Parking also possible in Lawrenny village.*

Please note: *The section along Garron Pill includes shore walking – check your tide tables as the shore will be under water at high tide!*

Going: *Easy.*

1. Lawrenny Quay

For centuries the sea and inland rivers have served as a magical highway for Pembrokeshire trade, commerce and communication. Viking raiders penetrated the Milford Haven as far north as Haverfordwest, whilst embattled Normans took care wherever possible to build their castles not only on strategic sites, but also on sites that overlooked or had access to the waterways of the Haven and the Daugleddau. From the Middle Ages onwards cargoes of coal, limestone, timber and grain set out from and arrived at

Lawrenny Quay

all ports of call on the river. In this atmosphere of bustle and activity Lawrenny's prosperity grew; it's quay was developed, and it's shipbuilding industry increased in importance. At nearby West Williamston, across the water at the junction of the Carew and Cresswell rivers, channels had been cut to give barges of 15 to 20 tons access to it's limestone quarries. Often the barges carried their loads to Haverfordwest, but it was usual to transship them at Lawrenny. A significant coal measure extended in a narrow strip from Saundersfoot to Nolton, passing to the north of Lawrenny. Those collieries of the Daugleddau Coalfield adjacent to the river established small quays for export. When visiting ships outgrew these quays, as they did at Cresswell and Landshipping, it became customary for barges to take the coal to Lawrenny, or nearby Llangwm, for reloading into waiting ships. It was for this purpose that Lawrenny's quay had been developed. People, as well as cargoes, were constantly on the move from Lawrenny Quay. Ferries took people and their wares down to Cosheston ferry and across to Roose ferry. The last ferry service continued until the 1960s.

At one time Lawrenny's shipyard was second only to Milford Haven's. From the 1800s through to the 1850s Milford built 91 ships; whilst Lawrenny's total was 61. The building of new towns downriver; Milford Haven from the 1790s, Pembroke Dock from 1814, and Neyland as the railway terminus from 1856, together with larger ships, spelt the end of village trade and quays. There was no shipbuilding at Lawrenny after thc 1850s. Lawrenny Quay now is a pleasant holiday site, catering to the boating and walking enthusiast, as well as the day tripper.

Benton Castle

2. The Daugleddau river and Benton Castle

The Daugleddau (*the two swords*) is strictly speaking that part of the river from the Cleddau Bridge to Picton Point, where the western and eastern swords join. The Daugleddau, with it's many small creeks, or pills, are a series of drowned river valleys, or rias, formed at the end of the Ice Age. The woodland is semi-natural oak, with the occasional wild service tree. Deciduous woodlands are now a rarity in Pembrokeshire and are found mainly here, on the banks of the Daugleddau, or further north in the Gwaun valley, near Fishguard. Steep valley slopes have been their best defence against farming. Benton castle, opposite, with it's smart coat of whitewash, dates from the 13th century, reputedly built by Bishop Beck of St David's. Substantially rebuilt in the 1930s, it is now a private residence.

3. Garron Pill

Garron pill is typical of the many small inlets on the river. From here the river's pattern of alternating low meadow land and steep wooded slopes abutting the shore becomes evident. The mudflats provide good feeding grounds for wildfowl and waders. Curlews, shelduck and teal compete with widgeon and mallard. The town of Llangwm, diagonally opposite, was famous in the 19th century for the quality of it's oysters. There have been recent attempts here to revive the industry by farming oyster beds on pontoons. These were set at the mouth of the pill, allowing for access at low tide. The women of Llangwm were noted in the county and South Wales for their individualism. At one time they used to row their menfolk downriver to work at the new towns, returning later in the day to collect them. They had their own distinctive fashion, and travelled from town to village selling the local fish and oysters. The wooden hut,

Garron Pill at high water

Lawrenny church

overlooking the pill, is used by the local scouts and guides. Coedcanlas, opposite, on Garron's side of the river, was the birthplace of Dick Francis, the author and jockey.

4.   Lawrenny Church
Lawrenny's fine church is the only one in the county dedicated to the 12th century Celtic saint Caradoc, who is known to have lived in Pembrokeshire. Originally late 13th century, a west tower was added in the 16th century. There are hand held information panels inside the church, which is well worth a visit.

5. Lawrenny Castle
Stunning views over Black Mixen below and the Carew and Cresswell rivers. The old limestone quarries at West Williamston opposite are now managed as a nature reserve. There have been two mansions here on this site. Early 18th century Lawrenny House was demolished to make way for Lawrenny Castle, a magnificent Victorian house dating from 1850, sadly demolished in the 1950s after failures to find a buyer. The Castle became the officer's mess during the Second World War when the Navy arrived with a seaplane training squadron in 1941. Lawrenny soon echoed to the sounds of Kingfisher and Walrus seaplane engines.

Walk directions: [-] indicates history note
1. Start from Lawrenny Quay [**1**]. Continue on the road

to the boat park. Cross to gain a woodland path.

2 Continue on the woodland track until, after a short distance, you reach a private house. Bear right and continue. There are fine views of the river and Benton castle opposite [2], before the path turns right inland by Garron pill [3].

Continue on the woodland path

3. Continue on the woodland path, passing the scout/guides hut, to reach a stile on your left. Cross the stile and follow the steps down to the shore. Turn right and continue inland along the shore.

4. At the minor road turn right and continue uphill to Lawrenny village.

5. Walk past the church entrance [4] and enter fields through a metal gate. Continue ahead, initially alongside a stone wall. Where the wall ends bear right uphill to reach a second metal gate.

6. Bear left and continue ahead, keeping the crenellated wall to your right. Above is the site of the now demolished Lawrenny Castle [5]. Keep ahead until the path bears left downhill through woodland to join the minor road opposite the Lawrenny Arms, continuing on to the quay.

Other information

BT telephone opposite the Yacht station. Quayside tearoom. Lawrenny village has a community shop/Post

View from site of Lawrenny Castle

Office mobile outreach service and BT telephone. Slipway at Lawrenny Yacht Station, which keeps some of it's moorings for visitors. Also caters for boat engine repairs. Youth Hostel in Lawrenny village.

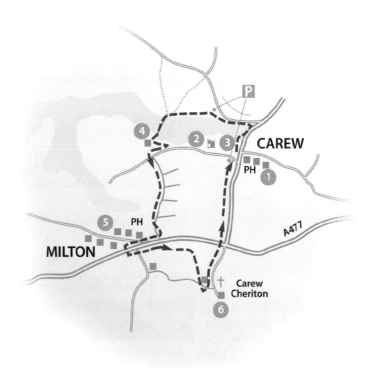

Walk 15
Carew and Milton

Walk details

Approx distance: *2.2 miles/3.5 kilometres*

Approx time: *1¼ hours*

O.S. Maps: *OS 1:25 000 South Pembrokeshire Outdoor Leisure 36*

Start: *Carew*

Access: *Carew is on the A4075, which itself leads off the A477 Pembroke Dock to Kilgetty and St Clears main road at Milton roundabout. Bus 360 Tenby to Carew and Milton, 361 Tenby to Pembroke Dock.*

Parking: *Car park opposite Carew Inn adjacent to the castle. Car park also by the mill pond itself – to reach cross the road bridge from Carew and turning left follow the minor road for a short distance, and limited parking possible in Milton.*

Going: *Easy – mostly on firm paths, a little road walking. Field paths by Milton.*

1. Carew Village

Like may other villages in the shade of a castle Carew's origins and prosperity would have grown with the history of the castle. Traders and craftsmen would have settled to help serve the castle and it's lord. The name Carew may derive from the Welsh *Caerau*, meaning forts – there are ancient prehistoric burial mounds in the area.

2. Carew Castle

Carew castle, in it's glorious strategic setting, is one of Wales' finest. It is believed to have been founded by Gerald de Windsor, castellan of Pembroke from 1093 to 1116. There

Carew Castle

were various additions over the centuries until circa 1480 Gerald's descendants sold it to Sir Rhys ap Thomas who enhanced the building, and is famed as the giver, in 1507, of the last great medieval tournament of Britain. Five days of feasting, harp music, and song were accompanied by contests of tilting, athletics, wrestling and deer hunting in the park, with evenings of theatricals and drinking. It is said a thousand men attended, and not a single fight or quarrel broke out!

On the impeachment of Sir Rhys's grandson the castle passed to Sir John Perrott, reputedly the son of Henry VIII. Lord Deputy of Ireland, and a Privy Councillor, he continued the castle's transformation into a brilliant Elizabethan palace, adding the superb North Gallery with it's mullioned windows. Turkish carpets, Irish rugs, silks, books and musical instruments and piped water were added to the interior. However before he could occupy it he was convicted of treason, and died in the Tower of London in 1592. After this great flowering the castle fell on hard times, suffering two sieges during the Civil War before falling into ruin. The castle is now open to the public Easter to October.

3. Carew Cross

Carew's magnificent Celtic Christian cross can be dated to 1035. It is a royal memorial to Maredudd, who with his brother Hywel, became joint ruler of Deheubarth (now south-west

Carew Cross

Wales) in 1033. Maredudd was killed in 1035. The inscription to him recorded on the front of the cross (facing the castle) reads MARGIT EUT REX ETG FILIUS – [*The cross of*] Maredudd (*Magriteut*) son of Edwin. It was moved to it's present position early in the 20th century; originally it was on a outcrop projecting into the road.

4. Carew Tidal Mill

In days gone by, when Carew French tidal mill was flourishing (French because it is believed French burr stones were used), steam barges and wooden sailing ships would have been seen heading up to the mill to deliver corn from Sandy Haven and other Milford Haven creeks, perhaps even from Bristol. The ground seed would have found local use. Nowadays the wide and shallow Carew river, home to curlew and shelduck, is only likely to play host to the occasional adventurous dinghy. There has been a mill upriver here since at least 1542, the present building dating probably from the early 19th century. The revival in agriculture of the late 18th century restored the fortunes of

Carew mill

the mill, however by 1937 operation had ceased. The earliest reference to the causeway itself dates from 1630, when it was noted that repairs had been made to it earlier in that century. Since restoration in 1972 Wales' only restored tidal mill can be visited from Easter to October.

5. Milton

Milton, or the mill settlement, dates from at least the 14th century. At it's centre would have been the grist, or corn mill, which continued in operation until the early 20th century – the walk passes by it's remains. The settlement was also involved in the production of textiles as there were also two carding mills in the vicinity, their historical presence noted both in Tudor times and in the 19th century. The distinctive red building visible from the walkway was the former waterworks and pumping station. Built in 1898 to

Milton

supply south Pembrokeshire it continued in operation until circa 1970. Milton's old road bridge, now pedestrianised, dates from 1820.

6. Carew Church

Earliest reference to the church dates from 1203, with the present chancel and transepts dating from 1326. It is an impressive building, with it's corner steeple it's most obvious distinction. The high altar was erected by public subscription to local men who fell during the 1914-18 war, the font, said to be an exact copy of an earlier Norman one, dates from the mid 19th century. The tower itself dates from just after 1500, however it needed repair after it was struck by lightning in 1926, costing an impressive, for the time, £1900. Effigies in the church include one of the Carew family in armour, dated to the late 13th/early 14th century. The church is dedicated to St Mary. The chantry chapel in the grounds, adjacent to the church path, was once used as a school, and a home for paupers. The church cemetery has war graves for those who were killed whilst serving at RAF Carew Cheriton during the 2nd World War, when Carew had it's own airfield.

Carew church and chantry chapel

Walk directions: [-] indicates history note

1. Starting from Carew [1] village walk down the hill past the castle [2] and Celtic cross [3] to reach the river and millpond, and after crossing the bridge turn left to reach the car park by the millpond.

2. Continue on the path alongside the pond, and cross the causeway left to reach the tidal mill [4].

3. Take the metal road leading away from the mill, to shortly turn right onto another metalled track. After a short distance cross a stone stile left.

4. Keeping to the left continue across fields to cross another stone stile on the left to enter a field. Bear right along the field edge to reach the main road.

Follow the path to reach a minor road

5. Turn right at the main road and continue on a path and crossing Milton's road bridge reach Milton [5] – Milton Brewery on right. Cross the main road and take the minor road opposite.

6. Just past the farm shop on the left turn left across a wooden footbridge and continue on a metal path, passing the ruins of Milton mill on your left. Follow the path to reach a minor road. Bear left and continue to Carew Cheriton and Carew church [6]. Once at the village bear left.

7. Continue on the minor road, again cross the main road, and keeping ahead return to the starting point.

Other information

Pubs in both Carew and Milton. Public toilets in Carew village, near the pub, and opposite the castle car park.

Carew castle holds a number of family oriented events

during the summer season, as well as daily guided tours.

Disused Carew airfield nearby has a Sunday market, and the recently restored Control Tower can currently be visited Sundays in July, August and September and on Bank holidays.

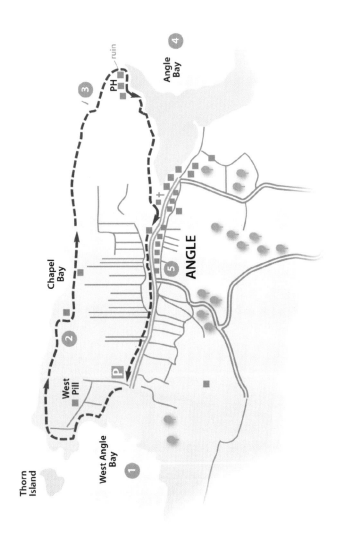

Walk 16
Angle

Walk details

Approx distance: *3.75 miles/6 kilometres*

Approx time: *2½ hours*

O.S. Maps: *OS 1:25 000 South Pembrokeshire Outdoor Leisure 36*

Start: *West Angle Bay*

Access: *Angle is reached on the B4320 from Pembroke, or via Castlemartin on the B4319. Follow the road through the village to reach West Angle Bay. Bus routes 387/388 the Coastal Cruiser Pembroke Dock – Stackpole – Angle.*

Parking: *Free car park at West Angle Bay.*

Please note: *At high tides the road to the Point House pub is under water for a short time.*

Going: *Easy – coastal path, some road walking.*

1. West Angle Bay

West Angle Bay is pleasant and attractive, with lots of sand, and plenty of rock pools for the young explorer. Situated as it is at the mouth of the Haven it has always played a part in it's defence. Following the scares of the Spanish Armada in 1588 Henry VIII had two defensive towers built, one, partly extant, on the eastern headland overlooking West Angle, the other, now vanished, on the opposite shore near St Ann's Head. Further 19th century fears, this time of French invasion, led to the establishment of an extensive system of defensible barracks and blockhouses. Often known as Palmerston's Follies, after the Prime Minister and Foreign Secretary of the time, there was a blockhouse, of which the gun emplacements remain, on the eastern headland, by Henry VIII's tower, and another on Thorn island.

West Angle Bay and St Ann's Head

Since the 1930s Thorn island's grey eminence has, though not at present, made a fine isolated hotel. During the Second World War Angle airfield was home to both spitfires and hurricanes. Operational from June 1941 to early 1943 there is a memorial plaque in the car park. Recent archaeological excavations on the headland to the left of the bay have revealed the presence of an early Christian burial ground, probably 9th or 10th century. It is believed a church dedicated to St Anthony once stood here.

Angle Brickworks flourished here from the 1870s, one of perhaps a dozen or so in the county. Producing bricks, tiles, and drain pipes, all that now remains is the brick chimney. To the right of the beach, just past the lime kiln, is an old limestone quarry. Providing stone for Thorn island, and lime for the brickworks and the land, there was at one time a tramway connecting quarry and brickworks, along the route taken by the present Coast Path. A passage blasted out on the seaward side has made it a sheltered harbour. There have always been wrecks around this dangerous

Thorn island and the Milford Haven

coast; one of the most famous being the *Loch Shiel*, en route from Glasgow to Adelaide Australia, with seven thousand cases of whiskey. Wrecked on Thorn island in

1894 the crew were successfully rescued by the Angle lifeboat; however only two thousand of the whiskey cases were officially recovered. Angle people are a hardy race! One more recent disaster was the oil tanker *Sea Empress*, holed on the Mid Channel rocks at the entrance to the Haven in February 1996, leaking seventy thousand tons of crude oil into the sea in the process. All visible traces of the oil spill were soon virtually eradicated from the local beaches, and the decline in the number of sea birds immediately after the spill proved to be temporary.

2. Chapel Bay fort

Built in 1890, and part of the haven's 19th century defences, there was a fort here at Chapel Bay, complete with an inland moat. The fort is currently the subject of a renovation project, with the ultimate aim of opening the site to the public. The line of the moat is clearly visible.

3. Angle lifeboat station

There has been a lifeboat at Angle since the 1860s. Originally known as the Milford Haven lifeboat the first station was built at Angle Point; the brick remains are all that are now left. The station moved permanently to it's present position in the 1920s. The current station dates from 1992, the lifeboat being the *Mark Mason*.

4. Angle Bay

The area between Angle, and, across the water, the inlets of Dale and Sandy Haven, is traditionally the best area in the haven for sea fishing, and Angle Bay has provided safe anchorage and shelter for countless fishermen and yachtsmen. The extensive mud flats provide important feeding grounds for wintering ducks and waders. The industrial complex across the bay is Valero's Pembroke refinery.

Angle Bay

Angle

5. Angle

Angle's long main street, with it's flat roofed houses, colonnaded former hotel, and scattered medieval buildings, has a distinctiveness unique in Pembrokeshire. Taking it's name from it's geographical position, in an "angle" of land, the village grew up around it's Norman landowners. Alongside the growing village were the strip fields which helped supply the Norman manor with food. These medieval strip fields are

Angle's Tower House

still there, and retain their original shape, stretched out as they are behind the houses on either side of the main street. The only difference now is that they are enclosed. Just north of the church is a 14th century sandstone tower house. Similar to tower houses in Ireland, Angle's tower house is unique in Wales. Above a vaulted undercroft are three storeys which would have been the living quarters. Access would have been at first floor level, thus allowing the occupants to seal themselves in should they be attacked. It was possibly the residence of the de Shirburn family, who were Lords of the Manor here from the late 13th to the 15th centuries. Usually open to the public. A short distance away, on private land, is a dovecote which would have provided plump pigeon pie for the table.

The church, dedicated to St Mary the Virgin, is 13th century, or at least the north wall and north transept are, the church was much restored in the 1850s. The tower is 15th century. There is a fishermen's chapel in the grounds. Dedicated to St Anthony it was built by Edward de Shirburn in 1447. There is also a tiered preaching, or Calvary cross, by the church entrance. Such crosses consist of a Latin cross mounted on three steps, symbolising Charity, Hope, and at the top, Faith. Just south of the main street, by the Post Office, is another medieval building. Marked as a fortified dwelling on OS maps there has been speculation that it may have been a nunnery. Certainly pilgrims sailed from West Angle Bay to Ireland, and across the Haven, near Dale, is Monk Haven, where pilgrims landed en route to St David's. Angle's distinctive flat roofed houses were built or restored at the end of the 19th century by the then owner of the Angle estate to remind him of the building style he had encountered on a tour of duty in South Africa. Nowadays Angle is very much a residential village, with some second homes.

Walk directions: [-] indicates history note

1. From West Angle Bay [1] follow the track to West Pill farm, shortly branching off to the left onto the Coast Path. Clearly signposted.

2. Continue on the Coast Path, passing opposite Thorn island, and then on past Chapel Bay fort [2] and Angle lifeboat station [3] to reach Angle Point and Angle Bay [4].

Past Chapel Bay fort

3. Passing the Old Point House pub continue along the track leading back to the village [5], and where the track branches left over a bridge go straight ahead.

4. Just past the medieval tower house go through a gate and walk diagonally left to reach a play area. Go through the play area to reach the main road through Angle.

5. Turn right and continue, passing the Hibernia Inn on the right, to West Angle Bay and the starting point.

Other information

Most facilities available in Angle. Two pubs – the Hibernia and the Old Point House. BT telephone, public toilets, café (under re-developments), and caravan park at West Angle Bay. Freshwater West, nearby, has one of the finest beaches and dune systems in the county, complete with renovated hut where edible seaweed was dried before being made into laver bread. Two feature films were partly shot at Freshwater West; Robin Hood with Russell Crowe, and Harry Potter and the Deathly Hallows. Can be a dangerous beach for inexperienced swimmers.

A complete walk around the Angle peninsula, utilising the footpath leading inland from just before Freshwater

West at Gravel Bay, is approximately 9½ miles/15½ kilometres. Well worth the effort!

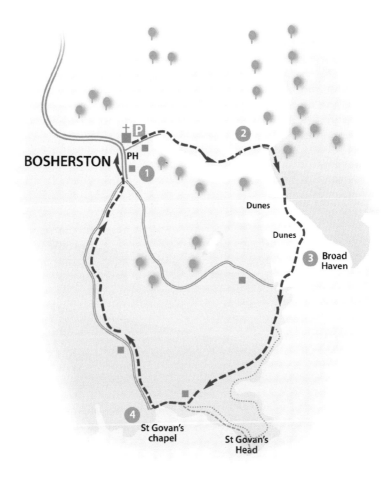

BOSHERSTON

PH

Dunes

Dunes

Broad
Haven

St Govan's
chapel

St Govan's
Head

Walk 17
Bosherston

Walk details

Approx distance: *4.25 miles/6.75 kilometres*

Approx time: *2½ hours*

O.S. Maps: *OS 1:25 000 South Pembrokeshire Outdoor Leisure 36*

Start: *Bosherston*

Access: *Bosherston is reached on the minor road from the B4319 Pembroke to Castlemartin road. Bus routes 387/388 the Coastal Cruiser Pembroke Dock – Bosherston – Angle.*

Parking: *Car park to the right of the church. Parking also possible at Broad Haven (seasonal charge), and at St Govan's Chapel.*

Please note: *Part of this walk is within the Ministry of Defence Castlemartin Range. Check in Bosherston, or with Tourist Information Centres, online Castlemartin Firing Notices, or phone 01646 662367 for Castlemartin Range Office recorded messages giving dates when firing is in progress and the Range closed. Red flags fly when Range in use.*

Going: *Easy – footpath, beach, field and grassland. Some road walking.*

1. Bosherston

A pretty place to while away a summer's afternoon, with the Olde Worlde Café and lily ponds nearby. Bosherston, Bosher's Town, was given to Bosher, in the retinue of de Stackpole who came over with William the Conqueror. In the 13th century it was known as Stackpole Bosher, to distinguish it from nearby Stackpole Elidyr. The church of St Michael and All Angels is late 13th century, built on the

St Michael and All Angels church

site of an earlier church. It was restored in 1855 by the
Cawdor family. The font is Norman. There is a preaching, or
Calvary cross, in the grounds, set into a three stepped stone
base representing from the top down faith, hope and charity
or love. The cross' probable date is 14th century. The head
at the intersection is probably that of Christ, and may
suggest that it was originally a crucifix that had been
mutilated during the Reformation, and, minus it's original
stem, been rediscovered and mounted on an upright of local
stone and converted to a Calvary cross. The church gateway
has what are known as *Cock and Hen* gateposts, formerly
common in the county at the entrances to farms and
churches. The two gateposts are topped by stones of
different sizes, the largest being the hen. The idea is
believed to be Viking in origin – they had the friendly habit
of displaying the heads of their enemies, male and female,
on their stockades.

2. Bosherston lily ponds

The lily ponds are an exhilarating area, particularly in May and June when they are at their best. A series of inter-connecting fish ponds comprising the western, middle and eastern arms they extend over some eighty acres and were created between the late 18th and early 19th centuries by the Earl Cawdor to enhance the Stackpole estate. The drowned river valley is protected from the sea by a shingle bank and sand bar, and as further guard against natural accidents, a man made retaining wall. The resultant freshwater pools provide good entertainment for coarse fishing; pike predominate, but there are plenty of perch, tench, eels and roach to try the temper. Three delightful footbridges give access. Well frequented by herons, swans, coots, mallards, moorhens and the occasional kingfisher, and otter. Lady Margaret's Seat, giving a grand view over the area, is a late 19th century obelisk with four stone seats built into it. There is a fine 3rd to 4th century BC Iron Age fort, known as Fishponds Camp, situated between the western and middle arms of the lily ponds. At that time the valley would have been open to the sea, and would have provided a good protected landing place for new settlers. The Stackpole estate is now under the care of the National Trust, the estate well worth exploring. New access paths are being opened up, it's woodlands under conservation and development.

Bosherston lily ponds

3. Broad Haven

Broad Haven is frequently called Broad Haven South to distinguish it from Broad Haven on St Brides Bay. It is a fine

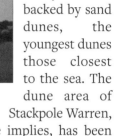

Broad Haven and Church Rock

sandy beach, backed by sand dunes, the youngest dunes those closest to the sea. The dune area of Stackpole Warren,

Dune orchids

as it's name implies, has been home to generations of rabbits, and it's warrens, both natural and artificial, were well used by rabbit catchers up until the 1950s. The Warren is still fed by sand blown up from Broad Haven – all dunes require dry sand, with sufficient wind to drive it ashore. Once these conditions are right then marram grass can send out it's roots, and the accumulations of sand colonised and stabilised. Dunes offer the opportunity to view the progression from bare ground through to stable dunes, and on to thin turf and thicket. Plenty of plant life to see, whether the blues of viper's bugloss or the red berries of sea buckthorn, and the purples of the orchids. The smaller of the two rocks guarding Broad Haven is Church Rock. It's profile, viewed from the car park area, bears an uncanny resemblance to King Kong. Good views from the sea's edge of the sheer cliffs of Stackpole Head and the softer outlines of Caldey island.

4. St Govan's chapel and Castlemartin peninsula

St Govan's chapel, built into the limestone cliffs at the only accessible point along this stretch of coast, has to be one of the best hermit's chapels in Britain. Despite legends connecting him with Sir Gawaine of Arthurian fame, St Govan is believed to be Gobhan or Gobban, the 6th century Abbot of Dairinis monastery in Wexford, Ireland. It is not known why he came to Pembrokeshire – perhaps there was a connection with St Ailbe, founder of Dairinis monastery, who originated from Solva, near St David's – whatever the reason he stayed the rest of his life in his cell in meditation and preaching. He died in 586. The present chapel dates from rebuilding in the 13th century (with a little recent help from the National Park), though the walls and altar may date from the 6th century. Of interest is the doorway to the north of the altar, which gives access to a small chamber cut into the rock. Outside the chapel there is a rock boulder known as Bell Rock. Legend tells that St Govan was given a silver bell which was stolen by pirates. St Govan duly prayed for it's return, and accordingly it was retrieved by angels and placed inside the boulder for safekeeping. The rock, on being struck by St Govan, gave out a note a thousand times louder than that of the original bell. To the south of the chapel there is a well, now dry, but which was visited until the 1850s for wishes and healing.

St Govan's chapel

The Coastguard lookout on St Govan's Head is only used in rough weather. The limestone cliffs from Linney Head to Stackpole Head are amongst the finest in Britain, and provide fine climbing opportunities. Cliff caves, still extant, were well favoured by late Mesolithic, Neolithic and Bronze Age peoples, who have left behind bones of red deer, wolf, pig and fox, as well as pottery, flint and the odd human bone as evidence of their presence. They may well have been good rock climbers, however access to the higher caves was easier then because the lower sea levels and the freezing and thawing of the rock face had resulted in cliff shattering, and the formation of rubble slopes, often reaching from the foot of the slope to the cliff top. Castlemartin peninsula came to the attention of the War Department in 1939, and the old storage magazines and some of the rails from that time are visible in the St Govan's Head area. After some fifty years as a Royal Armoured Corps range Castlemartin Range is now a field training centre for the Army. There are guided walks along the coast through the Range from Stack Rocks to Freshwater West, but given the extraordinary beauty and importance of the limestone cliffs they seem all too rare.

St Govan's Head and natural arch seen from the chapel

Walk directions: [-] indicates history note

1. Starting from Bosherston [**1**] head towards the church and the car park to it's right. Cross the car park and take the path leading downhill to the lily ponds.

2. At the first lily pond take the path bearing left and cross the footbridge.

3. Continue on the path leading around the pond to cross a second footbridge. The path from here ascends to meet a track. Bear right [**2**].

4. The path descends to a third footbridge. Turn right and cross the bridge (Grassy Bridge). Continue on the sandy path, keeping to the pond edge, to reach the junction of the lily ponds and Broad Haven.

5. Cross the footbridge to gain Broad Haven beach [**3**]. Keeping the outlet stream to your left either cross the beach or take a route though the sand dunes to gain Broad Haven car park. Steps will lead you up from the beach to the car park. Turn left and cross the car park to a field.

Wild garlic edging the path by Grassy Bridge

6. Bear right to Castlemartin Range entrance stile and gate. There is a Range hut, with warning notices clearly displayed. If there are red flags flying do not cross! Assuming all is well cross the Range. The path route is marked by signs marked *Danger – Military Firing Range – Keep Out* to keep you on the path, though a more dramatic route is to follow the path along the cliff edge, taking you across Trevallen Downs to the Coastguard lookout on St Govan's Head.

7. From the tarmac road leading to the Coastguard lookout continue, crossing by a cattle grid, to gain the access

Church Rock and St Govan's Head seen from Stackpole Warren

*Church Rock and Stackpole Head from the path by the
Range entrance*

point to St Govan's chapel [4] by the car park. Some seventy
four steps will lead you down – though legend has it that it
is impossible to count the same number of steps going back
up as were counted on the way down!

8. Return to Bosherston and the starting point along the
tarmac road leading inland away from the chapel and car
park. The road passes Royal Navy Control Tower Newton,
and a smaller Range hut, also *Newton*, both on the left
hand side.

Barafundle Bay

Other information

Pub (St Govan's Country Inn), public toilets, and BT telephone in Bosherston. Also a seasonal café – Ye Olde Worlde Café, and a Coastguard station (occasionally manned). Public toilets at Broad Haven car park. Emergency telephones at St Govan's Head (Coastguard lookout) and St Govan's chapel Range entrance. Coarse fishing permits are available from Ye Olde Worlde Café and National Trust office at Stackpole, as well as from wardens at lakeside.

Just a short distance along the Coast Path from Broad Haven towards Stackpole Quay is the fine sandy beach of Barafundle Bay, rightly known as one of Pembrokeshire's best. Access only possible on foot from either Broad Haven or Stackpole Quay.

Continuing on the Coast Path from St Govan's chapel (when the Range is open) will take you to the Green Bridge of Wales, a fine and large natural arch, one of the best sights of Pembrokeshire. Also close by the Green Bridge are the Elegug Stacks, or Stack Rocks, two limestone pillars which provide breeding sites for seabirds, in particular the guillemots – *gwylog* or *heligog* in the Welsh language. Access to the Green Bridge and Stack Rocks possible by road.

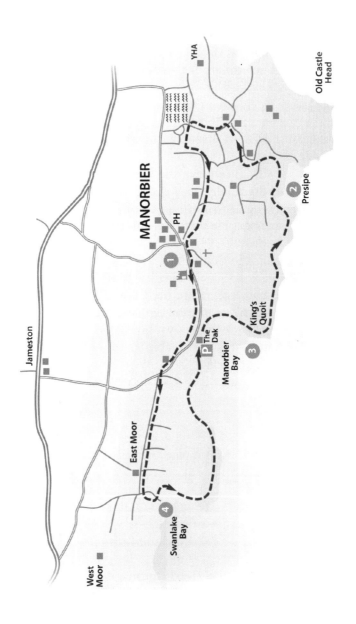

Walk 18
Manorbier

Walk details

Approx distance: *6 miles/9.5 kilometres*

Approx time: *3¼ hours*

O.S. Maps: *OS 1:25 000 South Pembrokeshire Outdoor Leisure 36*

Start: *Manorbier*

Access: *Manorbier is reached from the A4139 Pembroke to Tenby road, and is equidistant between the two towns. Bus 349 Tenby – Pembroke – Haverfordwest stops at Manorbier. Manorbier train station (service Swansea – Tenby – Pembroke Dock) is just over a mile/1.5 kilometres north of the village.*

Parking: *Either free parking in front of the Dak cottage overlooking Manorbier Bay, or in the National Park car park below Manorbier castle – seasonal charge. Parking also possible in Manorbier itself.*

Going: *Moderate. Coastal path, field, green lane and road – there is a fairly steep section at East Moor Cliff.*

1. Manorbier

The origin of Manorbier as a place name is uncertain. One interpretation has it as the *Maenor Bŷr*, that is a holding of land by Pyrrus or Pŷr, the 6th century first Abbot of Caldey island monastery. It is known that Caldey had farming estates on the mainland. Not much is known of Pyrrus, though it is known that after a night of too much local wine he drowned in the Abbey fishpond! The present spelling dates from the 1860s. The Norman history of Manorbier began when Odo de Barri was given lands here as a reward for military service, sometime shortly after the Norman invasion of Pembrokeshire in 1093. His son William began

Manorbier Castle

the building of the stone castle in the 12th century, though most of it's construction dates from between 1230 to 1260. More of a fortified mansion than a fortress new farming techniques were introduced which added new types of food, and a surplus for sale at that, to the oats, barley, meat and dairy produce normally consumed.

To the Norman colony were brought Flemish builders, farmers and tradesmen to supplant the local Welsh. An open field system was introduced, with water mill for grinding corn, fishpond, orchard, deerpark and dovecote added. The dovecote was renovated in 2013, and is reached on the footpath/road below the castle (located nearly opposite the National Park car park entrance). It is just past the ruins of a second, later mill. The original mill and fishpond were situated in the valley between the castle and the church. Manorbier castle was fortunate never to be attacked, partly due to the Welsh connections of the de Barris, partly because it was out of the way of the more imposing fortress castles. Nearly a ruin by the 19th century it was rescued in the 1880s by the talented renovations of JR Cobb.

The church across the valley is originally Norman, it's imposing tower dating from 1270. Dedicated to St James the

Great it was restored from 1867 to 1870. Worth a visit for it's unusual interior. Like many early ecclesiastical buildings it has a circular graveyard.

Manorbier church

Like it's near neighbours Tenby and Saundersfoot Manorbier's popularity as a seaside resort began from the mid 18th century and the building of the Pembroke to Tenby railway in 1863. Manorbier came to be seen as a little more exclusive than Tenby. In the centre of the village, opposite the Post Office, is the restored Bier House, nothing to do with the origin of the village's name, but built in 1900 to house the parish bier.

Manorbier's most famous son was born Gerald de Barri, son of William de Barri and Angharad de Carew, granddaughter of the last Prince of South Wales, Rhys ap Tewdwr, in circa 1146. Scholar, intellectual, politician and ecclesiastic, he was made Archdeacon of Brecon at 28, lectured in law at the University of Paris, and was chaplain and tutor to the young Richard I and King John. He spent much of his life campaigning to become Bishop of St David's and struggling with Henry II to create a Welsh National Church. His failure to do so was probably due him being too Welsh and too capable for Henry's uses. If this was not enough he still found time to pen seventeen books, of which the *Description of Wales* and *Journey through Wales*, and the *History and Topography of Ireland*, are the best known, and which are still in print. His life earned

Manorbier Bay and beach

him the title of Gerald of Wales, or Giraldus Cambrensis. He died in 1223, at the fine age of 77.

In his books he writes lively and entertaining prose, extolling the virtues of the Welsh, and his homeland of Wales and Manorbier. Here he is, in his Description of Wales from circa 1191, on the virtues of the Welsh, in this case their hospitality and generosity. *When you travel there is no question of your asking for accommodation or of their offering it: you just march into a house and hand over your weapons to the person in charge. They give you water so that you may wash your feet and that means you are a guest ... Guests who arrive early in the day are entertained until nightfall by girls who play to them on the harp ...*

2. Presipe

Presipe has a fine, sandy beach, with wonderful stratified sandstone cliffs. No access to it by car. The many stacks and rocks make it an interesting area for rock pool explorers, with plenty of sea anemones, crabs, starfish and those chameleons of the rock pool fish world, the blenny. The Atlantic gales and tides which hammer this southern coast can leave unusual visitors. I have seen jelly fish stranded by the tide, decked out in fine white, purple and yellow, with a thin, neat black line for a border, and tentacles splayed out on one side like silver chains. Old Castle Head, above, was once an Iron Age fort. During World War One airships, acting in accord with the hydrophone station on Carn Llidi on St David's Head, used to leave for photographic reconnaissance, on constant lookout for submarines. The site is now a Royal

Presipe

Artillery Range. Good views south to Lundy island on a clear day.

3. King's Quoit

King's Quoit is a Neolithic cromlech, or burial chamber, dating from circa 3,000 BC. Unusual, in that the main distribution of the cromlechs are on the northern coast, use may well have been made of a

King's Quoit

loose ledge from the ridge above to act as a capstone. However one of the three supporting pillars has fallen. There is no record of any skeleton being found. There have been both Mesolithic and Neolithic flint finds at Manorbier and around the headland at Swanlake Bay – the tides then would have been further out, away from the present shoreline, and at exceptionally low tides there are the remains of a prehistoric forest.

4. Swanlake Bay

Swanlake Bay, like Presipe, is another isolated beach, accessible only from the Coast Path, or on footpaths from East and West Moor farms. It's sandy beach and isolation make it a popular alternative

Swanlake Bay and East Moor Cliff

to the more crowded beaches of Freshwater East or Manorbier. Both East Moor and West Moor farms were original Norman land grant farms, under the lordship of Manorbier.

Walk directions: [-] indicates history note

1. From the National Park car park below the castle turn right on to the road and walk uphill towards Manorbier [**1**]. Ignore the first turning right to St James's church, instead continue and turn right by the Castlemead Hotel.

2. Follow the road past the houses onto a farm lane. Ignore the turning right and continue left to reach a stile giving access to a green lane – there is a good limekiln on the left just past the stile.

3. Continue straight ahead on the green lane to meet a short path bearing left uphill into a field.

4. Follow the path around to the right and cross the field to a road – there is a children's play area on the left here.

5. Turn right on to the road and continue uphill to turn right across a stile just before the boundary of Manorbier Royal Artillery Range – the road itself continues around left to Skrinkle Haven and the Youth Hostel. You are now on the Coast Path.

6. Follow the yellow waymarkers adjacent to the boundary fence, to cross two fields, and then turn left over a stile into a third field.

7. Go straight ahead, bearing slightly left, to reach the stile giving access to the cliff path.

Steps down to Presipe

8. Continue on the Coast Path, passing Presipe on your left [**2**] – steep steps will lead you down to the beach – and follow the Path for a mile/1.5 kilometres around to King's Quoit [**3**] and Manorbier Bay.

9. Cross Manorbier beach to cross a stream by a stone footbridge and climb the steps cut into the rock to gain the path passing in front of a parking bay.

10. Follow the path through the Dak grounds and continue on the Coast Path for well over a mile/1.5 kilometres to Swanlake Bay [4].

11. Cross the stile at the head of the beach and immediately turn right and follow the steep steps uphill to a field.

12. Keep to the right field edge, until just before a farm gate, cross a stone stile into another field.

13. Keep to the left field edge to meet a wooden stile into the farm lane at East Moor. Turn right, then shortly left to cross another stone stile.

14. Cross three fields, keeping to the left edge, to meet the minor road leading to Manorbier.

15. Turn right on to the road and follow it down to Manorbier and the starting point.

Surfers at sunset – Manorbier beach

Other information

Manorbier offers a Post Office and shop, BT telephone, and café, as well as the Castle pub. Public toilets by the castle entrance, and at the National Park car park. Manorbier castle and garden open daily Easter to September 30. Picnic site and Youth Hostel at Skrinkle Haven.

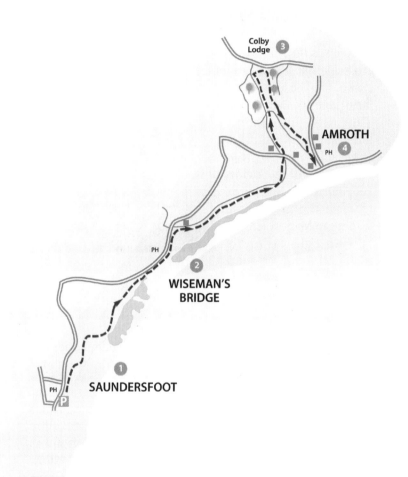

Walk 19
Saundersfoot to Wiseman's Bridge and Amroth

Walk details

Approx distance: *3.75 miles/6 kilometres*

Approx time: *2½ hours*

O.S. Maps: *OS 1:25 000 South Pembrokeshire Outdoor Leisure 36*

Start: *Harbour car park in Saundersfoot.*

Access: *Saundersfoot can be easily reached from the A478 Kilgetty to Tenby road. Accessible by train and a number of bus routes – once at Amroth bus 351 will take you back to Saundersfoot.*

Parking: *Fee paying car park at Saundersfoot harbour and Copper Hall, free at Amroth and Wiseman's Bridge.*

Please note: *At low tide it is possible to walk along the beach to Amroth; the beach route could be used to make a circular walk.*

Going: *Easy.*

1. Saundersfoot

One of Pembrokeshire's most popular holiday destinations the harbour and sandy beach are fine attractions. Geologically the area forms part of the South Wales coalfield, and the belt of coal running across Pembrokeshire from Saundersfoot to Landshipping, Hook and Nolton has come to be termed the Daugleddau coalfield. Records show coal mining dating back to at least the 14th century, with coal forming the major county export by 1700. However there was no attempt to exploit the potential of the local anthracite – amongst the finest in the world, and much

Saundersfoot

favoured by Queen Victoria for it's smokeless quality – until the 19th century. In 1829 the Saundersfoot Railway and Harbour Company was authorised, and by 1832 the harbour and one main line inland was in operation. Prior to the harbour's opening cargoes were loaded directly onto ships from the beach at Saundersfoot and Wiseman's Bridge. In 1842 the line was extended through three tunnels and along the cliff edge to Wiseman's Bridge, turning inland along Pleasant Valley to the Stepaside and Kilgetty collieries. Coal was hauled in drams by horse and oxen, until, in 1874, the line was re-laid and the locomotive *Rosalind* brought into service. The fortunes of the local collieries fluctuated, some closed, only to re-open, but by 1939 the coal industry here had ceased operations, and after 1945 the line was dismantled. Tourism is now the major industry. The last Pembrokeshire colliery to close was at Hook, inland on the river Cleddau, in 1949. The old railway line along the coast from Saundersfoot is now part of the Coast Path. To Wiseman's Bridge is a short 1 mile/1.75 kilometre walk, the tunnels cool and pleasant on warm summer days.

Oh yes, the origins of the name Saundersfoot; a reference to a property in the name of a local family, foot being in this case a topographical feature. Prior to industrialisation the town was no more than a handful of houses.

2. Wiesman's Bridge

Wiseman's Bridge takes it's name from one Andrew Wiseman who held half a knight's fee here, no Wiseman from the East this, but a Norman coloniser who reputedly accompanied an Earl of Pembroke, Aymer dc Valence, from Normandy to Pembrokeshire in the early 14th century. There is a fine pebble banked storm beach, with at low tide the superb expanse of golden sand stretching some three miles/five kilometres from Amroth to Saundersfoot. A full scale mock landing for D Day took place here in 1943, with landing craft, barges, guns and soldiers scattered

Wiseman's Bridge

along the sea-lashed beach from Pendine to Saundersfoot. Eisenhower, Churchill and Montgomery were on site to supervise, Churchill being properly entertained by the Wiseman's Bridge Inn with sandwiches, Welsh cakes and tea. An earlier army found a similar use for the beach, when in 1153 the sands and cliffs echoed to the march of a Royal army of the sons of the Prince of West Wales, en route to surprise and destroy the Norman garrison at Tenby. The present Coast Path along the cliff top was once the main county road from Saundersfoot to Amroth, but the collapse of iron ore workings in the cliffs below made the road impracticable.

3. Colby Lodge

Colby Lodge was built for the industrialist John Colby in 1803 to a Nash design. The woodland gardens were laid out by Samuel Kay, who bought the estate in the late 19th century. A good number of the original rhododendrons planted then, many brought back from the Himalayas by Kay's brother, have survived the years to grace the woodland slopes. The natural woodland here is believed to be a remnant of the great medieval forest of Coedrath which extended from Saundersfoot to Amroth. The timber would have been a useful source of fuel, the poor only using coal when they could not afford wood.

Colby Lodge

However with timber running short by the 1600s use would have been made of the local anthracite, and both anthracite and iron ore were extensively mined on the estate by John Colby during the early and mid 19th century. Some of the old workings can still be traced in the grounds, though little remains of the area's natural resources. Transport of coal from inland collieries to Saundersfoot harbour during their heyday in the 19th and early 20th centuries was, away from the railway lines, by carts, many pulled by teams of oxen and horses. As a result many roads were deeply rutted and often impassable. Turnpike Trusts were set up to improve conditions, but toll prices on the roads were so high that the local populace was alienated. Toll gates were smashed by rioters, that at nearby Killanow crossroads being no exception. The Killanow notice board, giving prices for animals, carts and men, has survived and has been on display at Colby Lodge's café. The gardens, though not the Lodge itself, are now in the hands of the National Trust, and is open during the summer season – many fine trees and vistas. The garden has two champion trees – a Japanese Red Cedar and a False Cypress, both being the tallest trees for their species registered in Britain and Ireland.

4. Amroth

The name Amroth (*Am-rath*) may mean on, or near, the river Rath, believed to have been the name of one of the parish's boundary streams, or on, or near the fort, and in various spellings can be traced back to at least 1220. Amroth's history as a village, however, dates back only as far as the mid 19th century. Prior to this a traveller journeying along the coast would have found only a scattering of houses near the church, or the gentry mansions. However Amroth was on the edge of the Daugleddau coalfield, and with 19th century industrial expansion both coal and iron ore were in

Amroth

demand. Between Amroth and Saundersfoot there were some fifty patches, each worked by two men who dug for iron ore in the cliffs. To exploit the iron the Pembrokeshire Coal and Iron Company opened an ironworks at nearby Stepaside in 1849. Stepaside Ironworks built up a reputation for quality, but by 1877 foreign competition proved too much and the ironworks closed. To the north of the village there developed the coal mining collieries of Coombes and Castlepark, small brothers of the larger Bonville's Court Colliery near Saundersfoot, and the Stepaside collieries, including Grove Colliery, opened to feed the ironworks. Amroth developed into a miners' village, close by the cliffs that gave many work.

The sea has always been jealous of the land here. Some 7,000 years ago there was a forest stretching far out from the present shoreline, the petrified remains still visible at exceptionally low tides. More recently, in the 1930s, the village at it's western end had houses on both sides of the road, but the storms soon put paid to their bright optimism, and they had to be demolished as unsafe. The present system of groynes along the beach are a modern attempt to further deny the sea. On clear days good views of Caldey island, Tenby and Saundersfoot on the right, with the Gower peninsula and the Worm's Head framing Carmarthen Bay to the left. Amroth castle, marked on the OS map, is recent, dating from the early 19th century, though it is on, or near the site of the Norman Eareweare castle, all traces of which have now vanished. The Norman castle was dealt a fatal blow by Prince Llywelyn, who in the early 1200s was in the process of reclaiming, albeit temporarily, much of South West Wales from Norman colonisers. Rebuilt at various times, and in various forms, the present castle has been converted to holiday flats, with caravans and chalets in the grounds. One early 19th century resident and local worthy rejoiced in the delightful title of the Reverend Thomas Shrapnel Biddulph. One wonders if his sermons were as explosive as his name might suggest.

Walk directions: [-] indicates history note

1. Starting from the harbour car park bear right to gain the Strand with it's many shops. Continue along the Strand (route of the old railway line) to leave Saundersfoot [1] through a series of tunnels to reach Coppet Hall and Wiseman's Bridge [2].

2. Walk past the Wiseman's Bridge Inn and continue uphill on the road, taking the first turning right. Shortly again turn right onto a No Through Road, to shortly gain a well defined track. Continue, passing a caravan park on the left. After just over ½ mile/¾ kilometre the Coast Path continues right over a stile. Continue instead ahead on the Public Path to reach the Amroth road.

3. Turn left, cross the road, and shortly turn right onto a Public Path, passing in front of houses. Continue past the houses to reach a grassy path. Good views of Colby Lodge ahead, in the trees. Continue ahead and downhill to meet a T junction of paths. Continue directly ahead to reach Colby Lodge [3] on your right.

4. Once at the lodge, either by walking right along the minor road or through the grounds, gain the other side of the building. Follow the path leading back the way you have come, but this time with the lodge to your right, to reach a minor road. Bear right to continue through Amroth [4] to reach the sea front by a bus stop, and by the Amroth Arms.

Other information

Most facilities available in Saundersfoot and Amroth. Pubs in Saundersfoot, Wiseman's Bridge and Amroth. Tea room, gallery and gift shop at Colby Lodge, as well as a walled garden with a fine gazebo.

Many of the buildings of Stepaside Ironworks and Grove Colliery have survived, though in a ruined sate – most impressive is the casting house. They can be found close to Stepaside; a short walk through Pleasant Vallcy, leading inland from Wiseman's Bridge, will take you to them.